BIBLE STORIES FOR YOUNG ONES

JESUS MY KING

*A read-along Bible storybook
on the Life of Christ*

THOMAS NELSON PUBLISHERS

Nashville

The following selections from the four Gospels include the major events in the life of the Lord Jesus Christ, in approximate chronological order.

The Bible used is the Contemporary English Version, an accurate translation of the original texts into natural, current English that readers of all ages can understand and enjoy.

The stories are illustrated by beautiful new watercolor paintings by artist Natalie Carabetta.

Whether they are being read to or are reading the stories themselves, children will be delighted with the vivid narration of these events from the greatest life ever lived.

Difficult phrases or passages are marked with a star (*) and are explained in *Notes* in the back of the book, where they are listed by page numbers.

CONTENTS

The Word of Life

(John 1.1-14)

In the beginning was the one
    who is called the Word.
The Word was with God
    and was truly God.
From the very beginning
    the Word was with God.
And with this Word,
    God created all things.
Nothing was made
    without the Word.
Everything that was created
    received its life from him,
and his life gave light
    to everyone.
The light keeps shining
    in the dark,
and darkness has never
    put it out.*
God sent a man named John,
    who came to tell
    about the light
and to lead all people
    to have faith.

John wasn't that light.
He came only to tell
        about the light.
The true light that shines
on everyone
        was coming into the world.
The Word was in the world,
        but no one knew him,
though God had made the world
        with his Word.
He came into his own world,
but his own nation
        did not welcome him.
Yet some people accepted him
        and put their faith in him.
So he gave them the right
        to be the children of God.
They were not God's children
by nature or because
        of any human desires.
God himself was the one
        who made them his children.
The Word became a human being
        and lived here with us.
We saw his true glory,
the glory of the only Son
        of the Father.
From him all the kindness
and all the truth of God
        have come down to us.

Some very wonderful things happened just before the only Son of God the Father became a human being.

An Angel Tells about the Birth of John
(Luke 1.5-25)

When Herod was king of Judea, there was a priest by the name of Zechariah from the priestly group of Abijah. His wife Elizabeth was from the family of Aaron.* Both of them were good people and pleased the Lord God by obeying all that he had commanded. But they did not have children. Elizabeth could not have any, and both Zechariah and Elizabeth were already old.

One day Zechariah's group of priests were on duty, and he was serving God as a priest. According to the custom of the priests, he had been chosen to go into the Lord's temple that day and to burn incense,* while the people stood outside praying.

All at once an angel from the Lord came and appeared to Zechariah at the right side of the altar. Zechariah was confused and afraid when he saw the angel. But the angel told him:

Don't be afraid, Zechariah! God has heard your prayers. Your wife Elizabeth will have a son, and you must name him John. His birth will make you very happy, and many people will be glad. Your son will be a great servant of the Lord. He must never drink wine or beer, and the power of the Holy Spirit will be with him from the time he is born.

John will lead many people in Israel to turn back to the Lord their God. He will go ahead of the Lord with the same power and spirit that Elijah* had. And because of John, parents will be more thoughtful of their children. And people who now disobey God will begin to think as they ought to. That is how John will get people ready for the Lord.

Zechariah said to the angel, "How will I know this is going to happen? My wife and I are both very old."

The angel answered, "I am Gabriel, God's servant, and I was sent to tell you this good news. You have not believed what I have said. So you will not be able to say a thing until all this happens. But everything will take place when it is supposed to."

The crowd was waiting for Zechariah and kept wondering why he was staying so long in the temple. When he did come out, he could not speak, and they knew he had seen a vision. He motioned to them with his hands, but did not say a thing.

When Zechariah's time of service in the temple was over, he went home. Soon after that, his wife was expecting a baby, and for five months she did not leave the house. She said to herself, "What the Lord has done for me will keep people from looking down on me."*

An Angel Tells about the Birth of Jesus

(Luke 1.26-38)

One month later God sent the angel Gabriel to the town of Nazareth in Galilee with a message for a virgin named Mary. She was engaged to Joseph from the family of King David. The angel greeted Mary and said, "You are truly blessed! The Lord is with you."

Mary was confused by the angel's words and wondered what they meant. Then the angel told Mary, "Don't be afraid! God is pleased with you, and you will have a son. His name will be Jesus. He will be great and will be called the Son of

God Most High. The Lord God will make him king, as his ancestor David was. He will rule the people of Israel forever, and his kingdom will never end."

Mary asked the angel, "How can this happen? I am not married!"

The angel answered, "The Holy Spirit will come down to you, and God's power will come over you. So your child will be called the holy Son of God. Your relative Elizabeth is also going to have a son, even though she is old. No one thought she could ever have a baby, but in three months she will have a son. Nothing is impossible for God!"

Mary said, "I am the Lord's servant! Let it happen as you have said." And the angel left her.

Mary Visits Elizabeth

(Luke 1.39-45)

A short time later Mary hurried to a town in the hill country of Judea. She went into Zechariah's home, where she greeted Elizabeth. When Elizabeth heard Mary's greeting, her baby moved within her.

The Holy Spirit came upon Elizabeth. Then in a loud voice she said to Mary:

God has blessed you more than any other woman! He has also blessed the child you will have. Why should the mother of my Lord come to me? As

soon as I heard your greeting, my baby became happy and moved within me. The Lord has blessed you because you believed that he will keep his promise.

Mary's Song of Praise
(Luke 1.46-56)

Mary said:

With all my heart
 I praise the Lord,
and I am glad
 because of God my Savior.
He cares for me,
 his humble servant.
From now on,
all people will say
 God has blessed me.
God All-Powerful has done
great things for me,
 and his name is holy.
He always shows mercy
to everyone
 who worships him.
The Lord has used
 his powerful arm
to scatter those
 who are proud.
He drags strong rulers
 from their thrones
and puts humble people
 in places of power.
He gives the hungry
 good things to eat,

and he sends the rich away
      with nothing in their hands.
He helps his servant Israel
and is always merciful
      to his people.
He made this promise
      to our ancestors,
to Abraham and his family
      forever!

Mary stayed with Elizabeth about three months. Then she went back home.

By this time we know that the Son of the Father would be named Jesus, which means "Savior." But he is also called Christ, which means someone especially blessed by God.

The Birth of Jesus
(Matthew 1.18-25)

This is how Jesus Christ was born. A young woman named Mary was engaged to Joseph from King David's family. But before they were married, she learned that she was going to have a baby by God's Holy Spirit. Joseph was a good man* and did not want to embarrass Mary in front of everyone. So he decided to quietly call off the wedding.

While Joseph was thinking about this, an angel from the Lord came to him in a dream. The angel said, "Joseph, the baby that Mary will have is from the Holy Spirit. Go ahead and marry her. Then after her baby is born, name him Jesus,* because he will save his people from their sins."

So God's promise came true, just as the prophet had said, "A virgin will have a baby boy, and he will be called Immanuel," which means "God is with us."

After Joseph woke up, he and Mary were soon married, just as the Lord's angel had told him to do. But they did not live together before her baby was born. Then Joseph named him Jesus.

During all this time a great ruler, named Augustus, reigned over the whole Mediterranean world. Mary and Joseph lived in that part of Augustus' empire called Galilee, a province in Palestine, but they had gone to the southern province of Judea when Jesus was born.

The Birth of Jesus
(Luke 2.1-7)

About that time Emperor Augustus gave orders for the names of all the people to be listed in record books.* These first records were made when Quirinius was governor of Syria.*

Everyone had to go to their own hometown to be listed. So Joseph had to leave Nazareth in Galilee and go to Bethlehem in Judea. Long ago Bethlehem had been King David's hometown, and Joseph went there because he was from David's family.

Mary was engaged to Joseph and traveled with him to Bethlehem. She was soon going to have a baby, and while they were there, she gave birth to her first-born* son. She dressed him in baby clothes* and laid him in a feed box, because there was no room for them in the inn.

The Shepherds
(Luke 2.8-21)

That night in the fields near Bethlehem some shepherds were guarding their sheep. All at once an angel came down to them from the Lord, and the brightness of the Lord's glory flashed around them. The shepherds were frightened. But the angel said, "Don't be afraid! I have good news for you, which will make everyone happy. This very day in King David's hometown a Savior was born for you. He is Christ the Lord. You will know who he is, because you will find him dressed in baby clothes and lying in a feed box."

Suddenly many other angels came down from heaven and joined in praising God. They said:

"Praise God in heaven!
Peace on earth to everyone
who pleases God."

After the angels had left and gone back to heaven, the shepherds said to each other, "Let's go to Bethlehem and see what the Lord has told us about." They hurried off and found Mary and Joseph, and they saw the baby lying in the feed box.

When the shepherds saw Jesus, they told his parents what the angel had said about him. Everyone listened and was surprised. But Mary kept thinking about all this and wondering what it meant.

As the shepherds returned to their sheep, they were praising God and saying wonderful things about him. Everything they had seen and heard was just as the angel had said.

Eight days later Jesus' parents did for him what the Law of Moses commands.* And they named him Jesus, just as the angel had told Mary when he promised she would have a baby.

Simeon Praises the Lord

(Luke 2.22-35)

The time came for Mary and Joseph to do what the Law of Moses says a mother is supposed to do after her baby is born.*

They took Jesus to the temple in Jerusalem and presented him to the Lord, just as the Law of the Lord says, "Each first-born* baby boy belongs to the Lord." The Law of the Lord also says that parents have to offer a sacrifice, giving at least a pair of doves or two young pigeons. So that is what Mary and Joseph did.

At this time a man named Simeon was living in Jerusalem. Simeon was a good man. He loved God and was waiting for God to save the people of Israel. God's Spirit came to him and told him that he would not die until he had seen Christ the Lord.

When Mary and Joseph brought Jesus to the temple to do what the Law of Moses says should be done for a new baby, the Spirit told Simeon to go into the temple. Simeon took the baby Jesus in his arms and praised God,

> "Lord, I am your servant,
>   and now I can die in peace,
> because you have kept
>   your promise to me.
> With my own eyes I have seen
> what you have done
>   to save your people,
> and foreign nations
>   will also see this.
> Your mighty power is a light
>   for all nations,
> and it will bring honor
>   to your people Israel."

Jesus' parents were surprised at what Simeon had said. Then he blessed them and told Mary, "This child of yours will cause many people in Israel to fall and others to stand. The child will be like a warning sign. Many people will reject him, and you, Mary, will suffer as though you had been stabbed by a dagger. But all this will show what people are really thinking."

❖ 13 ❖

Anna Speaks about the Child Jesus
(Luke 2.36-38)

The prophet Anna was also there in the temple. She was the daughter of Phanuel from the tribe of Asher, and she was very old. In her youth she had been married for seven years, but her husband died. And now she was eighty-four years old.* Night and day she served God in the temple by praying and often going without eating.*

At that time Anna came in and praised God. She spoke about the child Jesus to everyone who hoped for Jerusalem to be set free.

As we have seen, Emperor Augustus reigned over the Mediterranean world of that time. But he had appointed another king, Herod the Great, to rule over Palestine.

The Wise Men
(Matthew 2.1-12)

When Jesus was born in the village of Bethlehem in Judea, Herod was king. During this time some wise men* from the east came to Jerusalem and said, "Where is the child born to be king of the Jews? We saw his star in the east* and have come to worship him."

When King Herod heard about this, he was worried, and so was everyone else in Jerusalem. Herod brought together all the chief priests and the teachers of the Law of Moses and asked them, "Where will the Messiah be born?"

They told him, "He will be born in Bethlehem, just as the prophet wrote,

> 'Bethlehem in the land
>   of Judea,

you are very important
        among the towns of Judea.
From your town
        will come a leader,
who will be like a shepherd
        for my people Israel.' "

Herod secretly called in the wise men and asked them when they had first seen the star. He told them, "Go to Bethlehem and search carefully for the child. As soon as you find him, let me know. I want to go and worship him too."

The wise men listened to what the king said and then left. And the star they had seen in the east went on ahead of them until it stopped over the place where the child was. They were thrilled and excited to see the star.

When the men went into the house and saw the child with Mary, his mother, they kneeled down and worshiped him. They took out their gifts of gold, frankincense, and myrrh* and gave them to him. Later they were warned in a dream not to return to Herod, and they went back home by another road.

The Escape to Egypt
(Matthew 2.13-15)

After the wise men had gone, an angel from the Lord appeared to Joseph in a dream. The angel said, "Get up! Hurry and take the child and his mother to Egypt! Stay there until I tell you to return, because Herod is looking for the child and wants to kill him."

That night Joseph got up and took his wife and the child to Egypt, where they stayed until Herod died. So the Lord's promise came true, just as the prophet had said, "I called my son out of Egypt."

The Killing of the Children

(Matthew 2.16-18)

When Herod found out that the wise men from the east had tricked him, he was very angry. He gave orders for his men to kill all the boys who lived in or near Bethlehem and were two years old and younger.

So the Lord's promise came true, just as the prophet Jeremiah had said,

"In Ramah a voice was heard
crying and weeping loudly.

Rachel was mourning
> for her children,
and she refused
to be comforted,
> because they were dead."

The Return from Egypt
(Matthew 2.19-23)

After King Herod died, an angel from the Lord appeared in a dream to Joseph while he was still in Egypt. The angel said, "Get up and take the child and his mother back to Israel. The people who wanted to kill him are now dead."

Joseph got up and left with them for Israel. But when he heard that Herod's son Archelaus was now ruler of Judea, he was afraid to go there. Then in a dream he was told to go to Galilee, and they went to live there in the town of Nazareth. So the Lord's promise came true, just as the prophet had said, "He will be called a Nazarene."*

The Boy Jesus in the Temple
(Luke 2.41-52)

Every year Jesus' parents went to Jerusalem for Passover. And when Jesus was twelve years old, they all went there as usual for the celebration. After Passover his parents left, but they did not know that Jesus had stayed on in the city. They thought he was traveling with some other people, and they went a whole day before they started looking for him. When they could not find him with their relatives and friends, they went back to Jerusalem and started looking for him there.

Three days later they found Jesus sitting in the temple, listening to the teachers and asking them questions.

Everyone who heard him was surprised at how much he knew and at the answers he gave.

When his parents found him, they were amazed. His mother said, "Son, why have you done this to us? Your father and I have been very worried, and we have been searching for you!"

Jesus answered, "Why did you have to look for me?

Didn't you know that I would be in my Father's house?"* But they did not understand what he meant.

Jesus went back to Nazareth with his parents and obeyed them. His mother kept on thinking about all that had happened.

Jesus became wise, and he grew strong. God was pleased with him and so were the people.

After Augustus, a new emperor arose at Rome. Also, two sons of Herod the Great, Antipas and Philip, had come to power in Palestine. Antipas was known simply as "Herod," like his father.

The Preaching of John the Baptist
(Luke 3.1-20)

For fifteen years* Emperor Tiberius had ruled that part of the world. Pontius Pilate was governor of Judea, and Herod* was the ruler of Galilee. Herod's brother, Philip, was the ruler in the countries of Iturea and Trachonitis, and Lysanias was the ruler of Abilene. Annas and Caiaphas were the Jewish high priests.*

At that time God spoke to Zechariah's son John, who was living in the desert. So John went along the Jordan Valley, telling the people, "Turn back to God and be baptized! Then your sins will be forgiven." Isaiah the prophet wrote about John when he said,

> "In the desert
> someone is shouting,
> 'Get the road ready
> for the Lord!
> Make a straight path
> for him.

Fill up every valley
and level every mountain
and hill.
Straighten the crooked paths
and smooth out
the rough roads.
Then everyone will see
the saving power of God.'"

Crowds of people came out to be baptized, but John said to them, "You bunch of snakes! Who warned you to run from the coming judgment? Do something to show that you really have given up your sins. Don't start saying that you belong to Abraham's family. God can turn these stones into children for Abraham.* An ax is ready to cut the trees down at their roots. Any tree that does not produce good fruit will be cut down and thrown into a fire."

The crowds asked John, "What should we do?"

John told them, "If you have two coats, give one to someone who doesn't have any. If you have food, share it with someone else."

When tax collectors* came to be baptized, they asked John, "Teacher, what should we do?"

John told them, "Don't make people pay more than they owe."

Some soldiers asked him, "And what about us? What do we have to do?"

John told them, "Don't force people to pay money to make you leave them alone. Be satisfied with your pay."

Everyone became excited and wondered, "Could John be the Messiah?"

John said, "I am just baptizing with water. But someone more powerful is going to come, and I am not good enough even to untie his sandals.* He will baptize you with the Holy Spirit and with fire. His threshing fork* is in his hand, and he is ready to separate the wheat from the husks. He will store the wheat in his barn and burn the husks with a fire that never goes out."

In many different ways John preached the good news to the people. But to Herod the ruler, he said, "It was wrong for you to take Herodias, your brother's wife." John also said that Herod had done many other bad things. Finally, Herod put John in jail, and this was the worst thing he had done.

The Baptism of Jesus
(Luke 3.21-22)

After everyone else had been baptized, Jesus himself was baptized. Then as he prayed, the sky opened up, and the Holy Spirit came down upon him in the form of a dove.

A voice from heaven said, "You are my own dear Son, and I am pleased with you."

Now Jesus was faced with his first great trial. He would have to prove his authority as the Son of God.

Jesus and the Devil

(Matthew 4.1-11)

The Holy Spirit led Jesus into the desert, so that the devil could test him. After Jesus went without eating* for forty days and nights, he was very hungry. Then the devil came to him and said, "If you are God's Son, tell these stones to turn into bread."

Jesus answered, "The Scriptures say:

'No one can live only on food.
People need every word
        that God has spoken.' "

Next, the devil took Jesus to the holy city and had him stand on the highest part of the temple. The devil said, "If you are God's Son, jump off. The Scriptures say:

'God will give his angels
    orders about you.
They will catch you
    in their arms,
and you will not hurt
    your feet on the stones.'"

Jesus answered, "The Scriptures also say, 'Don't try to test the Lord your God!'"

Finally, the devil took Jesus up on a very high mountain and showed him all the kingdoms on earth and their power. The devil said to him, "I will give all this to you, if you will bow down and worship me."

Jesus answered, "Go away Satan! The Scriptures say:

'Worship the Lord your God
    and serve only him.'"

Then the devil left Jesus, and angels came to help him.

Not long after passing this great test, Jesus was proclaimed to be our Savior. This is exactly how it happened.

John the Baptist Tells about Jesus

(John 1.19-28)

The Jewish leaders in Jerusalem sent priests and temple helpers to ask John who he was. He told them plainly, "I am not the Messiah." Then when they asked him if he were Elijah, he said, "No, I am not!" And when they asked if he were the Prophet,* he also said "No!"

Finally, they said, "Who are you then? We have to

give an answer to the ones who sent us. Tell us who you are!"

John answered in the words of the prophet Isaiah, "I am only someone shouting in the desert, 'Get the road ready for the Lord!'"

Some Pharisees had also been sent to John. They asked him, "Why are you baptizing people, if you are not the Messiah or Elijah or the Prophet?"

John told them, "I use water to baptize people. But here with you is someone you don't know. Even though I came first, I am not good enough to untie his sandals." John said this as he was baptizing east of the Jordan River in Bethany.*

The Lamb of God
(John 1.29-34)

The next day John saw Jesus coming toward him and said:

Here is the Lamb of God who takes away the sin of the world! He is the one I told you about when I said, "Someone else will come. He is greater than I am, because he was alive before I was born." I didn't know who he was. But I came to baptize you with water, so that everyone in Israel would see him.

I was there and saw the Spirit come down on him like a dove from heaven. And the Spirit stayed on him. Before this I didn't know who he was. But

the one who sent me to baptize with water had told me, "You will see the Spirit come down and stay on someone. Then you will know that he is the one who will baptize with the Holy Spirit." I saw this happen, and I tell you that he is the Son of God.

The First Disciples of Jesus
(John 1.35-42)

The next day John was there again, and two of his followers were with him. When he saw Jesus walking by, he said, "Here is the Lamb of God!" John's two followers heard him, and they went with Jesus.

When Jesus turned and saw them, he asked, "What do you want?"

They answered, "Rabbi, where do you live?" The Hebrew word "Rabbi" means "Teacher."

Jesus replied, "Come and see!" It was already about four o'clock in the afternoon when they went with him and saw where he lived. So they stayed on for the rest of the day.

One of the two men who had heard John and had gone with Jesus was Andrew, the brother of Simon Peter. The first thing Andrew did was to find his brother and tell him, "We have found the Messiah!" The Hebrew word "Messiah" means the same as the Greek word "Christ."

Andrew brought his brother to Jesus. And when Jesus saw him, he said, "Simon son of John, you will be called Cephas." This name can be translated as "Peter."*

Jesus Chooses Philip and Nathaniel
(John 1.43-51)

The next day Jesus decided to go to Galilee. There he met Philip, who was from Bethsaida, the hometown of

Andrew and Peter. Jesus said to Philip, "Come with me."

Philip then found Nathanael and said, "We have found the one that Moses and the Prophets* wrote about. He is Jesus, the son of Joseph from Nazareth."

Nathanael asked, "Can anything good come from Nazareth?"

Philip answered, "Come and see."

When Jesus saw Nathanael coming toward him, he said, "Here is a true descendant of our ancestor Israel. And he is not deceitful."*

"How do you know me?" Nathanael asked.

Jesus answered, "Before Philip called you, I saw you under the fig tree."

Nathanael said, "Rabbi, you are the Son of God and the King of Israel!"

Jesus answered, "Did you believe me just because I said that I saw you under the fig tree? You will see something even greater. I tell you for certain that you will see heaven open and God's angels going up and coming down on the Son of Man."*

Jesus at a Wedding in Cana
(John 2.1-12)

Three days later Mary, the mother of Jesus, was at a wedding feast in the village of Cana in Galilee. Jesus and his disciples had also been invited and were there.

When the wine was all gone, Mary said to Jesus, "They don't have any more wine."

Jesus replied, "Mother, my time has not yet come!* You must not tell me what to do."

Mary then said to the servants, "Do whatever Jesus tells you to do."

At the feast there were six stone water jars that were

used by the people for washing themselves in the way that their religion said they must. Each jar held about twenty or thirty gallons. Jesus told the servants to fill them to the top with water. Then after the jars had been filled, he said, "Now take some water and give it to the man in charge of the feast."

The servants did as Jesus told them, and the man in charge drank some of the water that had now turned into wine. He did not know where the wine had come from, but the servants did. He called the bridegroom over and said, "The best wine is always served first. Then after the guests

have had plenty, the other wine is served. But you have kept the best until last!"

This was Jesus' first miracle,* and he did it in the village of Cana in Galilee. There Jesus showed his glory, and his disciples put their faith in him. After this, he went with his mother, his brothers, and his disciples to the town of Capernaum, where they stayed for a few days.

In order to show what it means to worship God truly, Jesus also had to show what false worship is. He chose the greatest festival of his time to teach us the meaning of true worship.

Jesus in the Temple
(John 2.13-22)

Not long before the Jewish festival of Passover, Jesus went to Jerusalem. There he found people selling cattle, sheep, and doves in the temple. He also saw moneychangers sitting at their tables. So he took some rope and made a whip. Then he chased everyone out of the temple, together with their sheep and cattle. He turned over the tables of the moneychangers and scattered their coins.

Jesus said to the people who had been selling doves, "Get those doves out of here! Don't make my Father's house a marketplace."

The disciples then remembered that the Scriptures say, "My love for your house burns in me like a fire."

The Jewish leaders asked Jesus, "What miracle* will you work to show us why you have done this?"

"Destroy this temple," Jesus answered, "and in three days I will build it again!"

The leaders replied, "It took forty-six years to build this temple. What makes you think you can rebuild it in three days?"

But Jesus was talking about his body as a temple. And when he was raised from death, his disciples remembered what he had told them. Then they believed the Scriptures and the words of Jesus.

Jesus Knows What People Are Like
(John 2.23-25)

In Jerusalem during Passover many people put their faith in Jesus, because they saw him work miracles.* But Jesus knew what was in their hearts, and he would not let them have power over him. No one had to tell him what people were like. He already knew.

As we have just seen, people didn't always come to Jesus with sincere faith. All the same, Jesus sought and found many who accepted him with all their hearts.

Jesus and Nicodemus
(John 3.1-21)

There was a man named Nicodemus who was a Pharisee and a Jewish leader. One night he went to Jesus and said, "Sir, we know that God has sent you to teach us. You could not work these miracles, unless God were with you."

Jesus replied, "I tell you for certain that you must be born from above* before you can see God's kingdom!"

Nicodemus asked, "How can a grown man ever be born a second time?"

Jesus answered:

I tell you for certain that before you can get into God's kingdom, you must be born not only by water, but by the Spirit. Humans give life to their children. Yet only God's Spirit can change you into a child of God. Don't be surprised when I say that you must be born from above. Only God's Spirit gives new life. The Spirit is like the wind that blows wherever it wants to. You can hear the wind, but you don't know where it comes from or where it is going.

"How can this be?" Nicodemus asked.

Jesus replied:

How can you be a teacher of Israel and not know these things? I tell you for certain that we know what we are talking about because we have seen it ourselves. But none of you will accept what we say. If you don't believe when I talk to you about things on earth, how can you possibly believe if I talk to you about things in heaven?

No one has gone up to heaven except the Son of Man, who came down from there. And the Son of Man must be lifted up, just as that metal snake was lifted up by Moses in the desert.* Then everyone who has faith in the Son of Man will have eternal life.

God loved the people of this world so much that he gave his only Son, so that everyone who has faith in him will have eternal life and never die. God did not send his Son into the world to condemn its people. He sent him to save them! No one who has faith in God's Son will be condemned. But everyone who does not have faith in him has already been condemned for not having faith in God's only Son.

The light has come into the world, and people who do evil things are judged guilty because they love the dark more than the light. People who do evil hate the light and won't come to the light, because it clearly shows what they have done. But everyone who lives by the truth will come to the light, because they want others to know that God is really the one doing what they do.

Jesus and the Samaritan Woman

(John 4.3-42)

Jesus left Judea and started for Galilee again. This time he had to go through Samaria, and on his way he came to the town of Sychar. It was near the field that Jacob had long ago given to his son Joseph. The well that Jacob had dug was still there, and Jesus sat down beside it because he was tired from traveling. It was noon, and after Jesus' disciples had gone into town to buy some food, a Samaritan woman came to draw water from the well.

Jesus asked her, "Would you please give me a drink of water?"

"You are a Jew," she replied, "and I am a Samaritan woman. How can you ask me for a drink of water when Jews and Samaritans won't have anything to do with each other?"*

Jesus answered, "You don't know what God wants to give you, and you don't know who is asking you for a drink. If you did, you would ask him for the water that gives life."

"Sir," the woman said, "you don't even have a bucket, and the well is deep. Where are you going to get this life-giving water? Our ancestor Jacob dug this well for us, and his family and animals got water from it. Are you greater than Jacob?"

Jesus answered, "Everyone who drinks this water will get thirsty again. But no one who drinks the water I give will ever be thirsty again. The water I give is like a flowing fountain that gives eternal life."

The woman replied, "Sir, please give me a drink of that water! Then I won't have to come to this well again."

Jesus told her, "Go and bring your husband."

The woman answered, "I don't have a husband."

"That's right," Jesus replied, "you're telling the truth. You don't have a husband. You have already been married five times, and the man you are now living with is not your husband."

The woman said, "Sir, I can see that you are a prophet. My ancestors worshiped on this mountain,* but you Jews say Jerusalem is the only place to worship."

Jesus said to her:

Believe me, the time is coming when you won't worship God either on this mountain or in Jerusalem. You Samaritans don't really know the one you worship. But we Jews do know the God we worship, and by using us God will save the world. But a time is coming, and it is already here! Even now the true worshipers are being led by the Spirit to worship the Father according to the truth. These are the ones the Father is seeking to worship him. God is Spirit, and those who worship God must be led by the Spirit to worship him according to the truth.

The woman said, "I know that the Messiah will come. He is the one we call Christ. When he comes, he will explain everything to us."

"I am that one," Jesus told her, "and I am speaking to you now."

The disciples returned about this time and were surprised to find Jesus talking with a woman. But none of them asked him what he wanted or why he was talking with her.

The woman left her water jar and ran back into town. She said to the people, "Come and see a man who told me everything I have ever done! Could he be the Messiah?" Everyone in town went out to see Jesus.

While this was happening, Jesus' disciples were saying to him, "Teacher, please eat something."

But Jesus told them, "I have food that you don't know anything about."

His disciples started asking each other, "Has someone brought him something to eat?"

Jesus said:

My food is to do what God wants! He is the one who sent me, and I must finish the work that he gave me to do. You may say that there are still four months until harvest time. But I tell you to look, and you will see that the fields are ripe and ready to harvest.

Even now the harvest workers are receiving their reward by gathering a harvest that brings eternal life. Then everyone who planted the seed and everyone who harvests the crop will celebrate together. So the saying proves true, "Some plant the seed, and others harvest the crop." I am sending you to harvest crops in fields where others have done all the hard work.

A lot of Samaritans in that town put their faith in Jesus because the woman had said, "This man told me everything I have ever done." They came and asked him to stay in their town, and he stayed on for two days.

Many more Samaritans put their faith in Jesus because of what they heard him say. They told the woman, "We no longer have faith in Jesus just because of what you told us. We have heard him ourselves, and we are certain that he is the Savior of the world!"

After his trip to Jerusalem to attend the Passover festival, and his stopover in Samaria, Jesus returned to his home in the province of Galilee.

The People of Nazareth Turn against Jesus
(Luke 4.16-30)

Jesus went back to Nazareth, where he had been brought up, and as usual he went to the meeting place on the Sabbath. When he stood up to read from the Scriptures, he was given the book of Isaiah the prophet. He opened it and read,

> "The Lord's Spirit
>> has come to me,
> because he has chosen me
> to tell the good news
>> to the poor.
> The Lord has sent me
> to announce freedom
>> for prisoners,
> to give sight to the blind,

> to free everyone
>> who suffers,
> and to say, 'This is the year
>> the Lord has chosen.'"

Jesus closed the book, then handed it back to the man in charge and sat down. Everyone in the meeting place looked straight at Jesus.

Then Jesus said to them, "What you have just heard me read has come true today."

All the people started talking about Jesus and were amazed at the wonderful things he said. They kept on asking, "Isn't he Joseph's son?"

Jesus answered:

> You will certainly want to tell me this saying, "Doctor, first make yourself well." You will tell me to do the same things here in my own hometown that you heard I did in Capernaum. But you can be sure that no prophets are liked by the people of their own hometown.

> Once during the time of Elijah there was no rain for three and a half years, and people everywhere were starving. There were many widows in Israel, but Elijah was sent only to a widow in the town of Zarephath near the city of Sidon. During the time of the prophet Elisha, many men in Israel had leprosy.* But no one was healed, except Naaman who lived in Syria.

When the people in the meeting place heard Jesus say this, they became so angry that they got up and threw him out of town. They dragged him to the edge of the cliff on which the town was built, because they wanted to throw him down from there. But Jesus slipped through the crowd and got away.

Jesus Heals Many People
(Mark 1.29-39)

As soon as Jesus left the meeting place with James and John, they went home with Simon and Andrew. When they got there, Jesus was told that Simon's mother-in-law was sick in bed with fever. Jesus went to her. He took hold of her hand and helped her up. The fever left her, and she served them a meal.

That evening after sunset,* all who were sick or had demons in them were brought to Jesus. In fact, the whole town gathered around the door of the house. Jesus healed all kinds of terrible diseases and forced out a lot of demons. But the demons knew who he was, and he did not let them speak.

Very early the next morning Jesus got up and went to a place where he could be alone and pray. Simon and the others started looking for him. And when they found him, they said, "Everyone is looking for you!"

Jesus replied, "We must go to the nearby towns, so that I can tell the good news to those people. This is why I have come." Then Jesus went to Jewish meeting places everywhere in Galilee, where he preached and forced out demons.

Jesus taught some very interesting things about how the Lord's special day of rest should be kept.

Jesus Heals a Sick Man

(John 5.1-18)

Later, Jesus went to Jerusalem for another Jewish festival.* In the city near the sheep gate was a pool with five porches, and its name in Hebrew was Bethzatha.*

Many sick, blind, lame, and crippled people were lying close to the pool.*

Beside the pool was a man who had been sick for thirty-eight years. When Jesus saw the man and realized that he had been crippled for a long time, he asked him, "Do you want to be healed?"

The man answered, "Lord, I don't have anyone to put me in the pool when the water is stirred up. I try to get in, but someone else always gets there first."

Jesus told him, "Pick up your mat and walk!" Right then the man was healed. He picked up his mat and started walking around. The day on which this happened was a Sabbath.

When the Jewish leaders saw the man carrying his mat, they said to him, "This is the Sabbath! No one is allowed to carry a mat on the Sabbath."

But he replied, "The man who healed me told me to pick up my mat and walk."

They asked him, "Who is this man that told you to pick up your mat and walk?" But he did not know who Jesus was, and Jesus had left because of the crowd.

Later, Jesus met the man in the temple and told him, "You are now well. But don't sin anymore or something worse might happen to you." The man left and told the leaders that Jesus was the one who had healed him. They started making a lot of trouble for Jesus because he did things like this on the Sabbath.

But Jesus said, "My Father has never stopped working, and that is why I keep on working." Now the leaders wanted to kill Jesus for two reasons. First, he had broken the law of the Sabbath. But even worse, he had said that God was his Father, which made him equal with God.

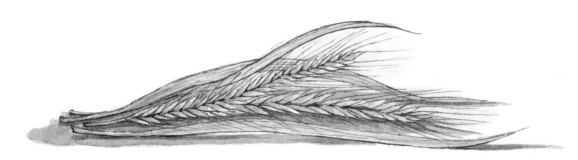

A Question about the Sabbath
(Luke 6.1-5)

One Sabbath when Jesus and his disciples were walking through some wheat fields,* the disciples picked some wheat. They rubbed the husks off with their hands and started eating the grain.

Some Pharisees said, "Why are you picking grain on the Sabbath? You're not supposed to do that!"

Jesus answered, "You surely have read what David did when he and his followers were hungry. He went into the house of God and took the sacred loaves of bread that only priests were supposed to eat. He not only ate some himself, but even gave some to his followers."

Jesus finished by saying, "The Son of Man is Lord over the Sabbath."

Jesus showed that everyone has special work to do for him.

Jesus Chooses His Twelve Apostles
(Mark 3.13-19)

Jesus decided to ask some of his disciples to go up on a mountain with him, and they went. Then he chose twelve of them to be his apostles,* so that they could be with him. He also wanted to send them out to preach and to force out demons. Simon was one of the twelve, and Jesus named him Peter. There were also James and John, the two sons of Zebedee. Jesus called them Boanerges, which means "Thunderbolts." Andrew, Philip, Bartholomew, Matthew, Thomas, James son of Alphaeus, and Thaddaeus were also apostles. The others were Simon, known as the Eager One,* and Judas Iscariot,* who later betrayed Jesus.

Back in his own country of Galilee, Jesus took time to teach and show examples of his ideas for his great new society.

The Sermon on the Mount
(Matthew 5.1—7.29)

When Jesus saw the crowds, he went up on the side of a mountain and sat down.*

Blessings

Jesus' disciples gathered around him, and he taught them:

God blesses those people
      who depend only on him.
They belong to the kingdom
      of heaven!*
God blesses those people
who grieve.
      They will find comfort!
God blesses those people
      who are humble.
The earth will belong
      to them!
God blesses those people
who want to obey him*
      more than to eat or drink.
They will be given
      what they want!
God blesses those people
      who are merciful.
They will be treated
      with mercy!
God blesses those people
whose hearts are pure.
      They will see him!
God blesses those people
      who make peace.
They will be called
      his children!
God blesses those people
who are treated badly
      for doing right.
They belong to the kingdom
      of heaven.*

God will bless you when people insult you, mistreat you, and tell all kinds of evil lies about you because of me. Be happy and excited! You will have a great reward in heaven. People did these same things to the prophets who lived long ago.

Salt and Light

You are like salt for everyone on earth. But if salt no longer tastes like salt, how can it make food salty? All it is good for is to be thrown out and walked on.

You are like light for the whole world. A city built on top of a hill cannot be hidden, and no one would light a lamp and put it under a clay pot. A lamp is placed on a lamp stand, where it can give light to everyone in the house. Make your light shine, so that others will see the good that you do and will praise your Father in heaven.

The Law of Moses

Don't suppose that I came to do away with the Law and the Prophets.* I did not come to do away

with them, but to give them their full meaning. Heaven and earth may disappear. But I promise you that not even a period or comma will ever disappear from the Law. Everything written in it must happen.

If you reject even the least important command in the Law and teach others to do the same, you will be the least important person in the kingdom of heaven. But if you obey and teach others its commands, you will have an important place in the kingdom. You must obey God's commands better than the Pharisees and the teachers of the Law obey them. If you don't, I promise you that you will never get into the kingdom of heaven.

Anger

You know that our ancestors were told, "Do not murder" and "A murderer must be brought to trial." But I promise you that if you are angry with someone,* you will have to stand trial. If you call someone a fool, you will be taken to court. And if you say that someone is worthless, you will be in danger of the fires of hell.

So if you are about to place your gift on the altar and remember that someone is angry with you, leave your gift there in front of the altar. Make peace with that person, then come back and offer your gift to God.

Before you are dragged into court, make friends with the person who has accused you of doing wrong. If you don't, you will be handed over to the judge and then to the officer who will put you in jail. I promise you that you will not get out until you have paid the last cent you owe.

Marriage

You know the commandment which says, "Be faithful in marriage." But I tell you that if you look at another woman and want her, you are already unfaithful in your thoughts. If your right eye causes you to sin, poke it out and throw it away. It is better to lose one part of your body, than for your whole body to end up in hell. If your right hand causes you to sin, chop it off and throw it away! It is better to lose one part of your body, than for your whole body to be thrown into hell.

Divorce

You have been taught that a man who divorces his wife must write out divorce papers for her.* But I tell you not to divorce your wife unless she has committed some terrible sexual sin.* If you divorce her, you will cause her to be unfaithful, just as any man who marries her is guilty of taking another man's wife.

Promises

You know that our ancestors were told, "Don't use the Lord's name to make a promise unless you are going to keep it." But I tell you not to swear by anything when you make a promise! Heaven is God's throne, so don't swear by heaven. The earth is God's footstool, so don't swear by the earth. Jerusalem is the city of the great king, so don't swear by it. Don't swear by your own head. You cannot make one hair white or black. When you make a promise, say only "Yes" or "No." Anything else comes from the devil.

Revenge

You know that you have been taught, "An eye for an eye and a tooth for a tooth." But I tell you not to try to get even with a person who has done something to you. When someone slaps your right cheek,* turn and let that person slap your other cheek. If someone sues you for your shirt, give up your coat as well. If a soldier forces you to carry his pack one mile, carry it two miles.* When people ask you for something, give it to them. When they want to borrow money, loan it to them.

Love

You have heard people say, "Love your neighbors and hate your enemies." But I tell you to love your enemies and pray for anyone who mistreats you. Then you will be acting like your Father in heaven. He makes the sun rise on both good and bad people. And he sends rain for the ones who do right and for the ones who do wrong. If you love only those people who love you, will God reward you for that? Even tax collectors* love their friends. If you greet only your friends, what's so great about that? Don't even unbelievers do that? But you must always act like your Father in heaven.

Giving

When you do good deeds, don't try to show off. If you do, you won't get a reward from your Father in heaven.

When you give to the poor, don't blow a loud horn. That's what showoffs do in the meeting places and on the street corners, because they are always looking for praise. I promise you that they already have their reward.

When you give to the poor, don't let anyone know about it.* Then your gift will be given in secret. Your Father knows what is done in secret, and he will reward you.

Prayer

When you pray, don't be like those showoffs who love to stand up and pray in the meeting places and on the street corners. They do this just to look good. I promise you that they already have their reward.

When you pray, go into a room alone and close the door. Pray to your Father in private. He knows what is done in private, and he will reward you.

When you pray, don't talk on and on as people do who don't know God. They think God likes to hear long prayers. Don't be like them. Your Father knows what you need before you ask.

You should pray like this:
Our Father in heaven,
    help us to honor your name.
Come and set up your kingdom,
so that everyone on earth
    will obey you,
as you are obeyed
    in heaven.
Give us our food for today.*
Forgive our sins,
    as we forgive others.*
Keep us from being tempted
    and protect us from evil.*

If you forgive others for the wrongs they do to you, your Father in heaven will forgive you. But if you don't forgive others, your Father will not forgive your sins.

Worshiping God by Going without Eating

When you go without eating,* don't try to look gloomy as those showoffs do when they go without eating. I promise you that they already have their reward. Instead, comb your hair and wash your face. Then others won't know that you are going without eating. But your Father sees what is done in private, and he will reward you.

Treasures in Heaven

Don't store up treasures on earth! Moths and rust can destroy them, and thieves can break in and steal them. Instead, store up your treasures in heaven, where moths and rust cannot destroy them, and thieves cannot break in and steal them. Your heart will always be where your treasure is.

Light

Your eyes are like a window for your body. When they are good, you have all the light you need. But when your eyes are bad, everything is dark. If the light inside you is dark, you surely are in the dark.

Money

You cannot be the slave of two masters! You will like one more than the other or be more loyal to one than the other. You cannot serve both God and money.

Worry

I tell you not to worry about your life. Don't worry about having something to eat, drink, or wear. Isn't life more than food or clothing? Look at the birds in the sky! They don't plant or harvest. They don't even store grain in barns. Yet your Father in heaven takes care of them. Aren't you worth more than birds?

Can worry make you live longer?* Why worry about clothes? Look how the wild flowers grow. They don't work hard to make their clothes. But I tell you that Solomon with all his wealth* was not as well clothed as one of them. God gives such beauty to everything that grows in the fields, even though it is here today and thrown into a fire tomorrow. He will surely do even more for you! Why do you have such little faith?

Don't worry and ask yourselves, "Will we have anything to eat? Will we have anything to drink? Will we have any clothes to wear?" Only people who don't know God are always worrying about such things. Your Father in heaven knows that you need all of these. But more than anything else, put God's work first and do what he wants. Then all the other things will be yours as well.

Don't worry about tomorrow. It will take care of itself. You have enough to worry about today.

Judging Others

Don't condemn others, and God will not condemn you. God will be as hard on you as you are on others! He will treat you exactly as you treat them.

You can see the speck in your friend's eye, but you don't notice the log in your own eye. How can you say, "My friend, let me take the speck out of your eye," when you don't see the log in your own eye? You're nothing but showoffs! First, take the log out of your own eye. Then you can see how to take the speck out of your friend's eye.

Don't give to dogs what belongs to God. They will only turn and attack you. Don't throw pearls down in front of pigs. They will trample all over them.

Ask, Search, Knock

Ask, and you will receive. Search, and you will find. Knock, and the door will be opened for you. Everyone who asks will receive. Everyone who searches will find. And the door will be opened for everyone who knocks. Would any of you give your hungry child a stone, if the child asked for some bread? Would you give your child a snake if the child asked for a fish? As bad as you are, you still know how to give good gifts to your children. But your heavenly Father is even more ready to give good things to people who ask.

Treat others as you want them to treat you. This is what the Law and the Prophets* are all about.

The Narrow Gate

Go in through the narrow gate. The gate to destruction is wide, and the road that leads there is easy to follow. A lot of people go through that gate. But the gate to life is very narrow. The road that leads there is so hard to follow that only a few people find it.

A Tree and Its Fruit

Watch out for false prophets! They dress up like sheep, but inside they are wolves who have come to attack you. You can tell what they are by what they do. No one picks grapes or figs from thorn bushes. A good tree produces good fruit, and a bad tree produces bad fruit. A good tree cannot produce bad fruit, and a bad tree cannot produce good fruit. Every tree that produces bad fruit will be chopped down and burned. You can tell who the false prophets are by their deeds.

A Warning

Not everyone who calls me their Lord will get into the kingdom of heaven. Only the ones who obey my Father in heaven will get in. On the day of judgment many will call me their Lord. They will say, "We preached in your name, and in your name we forced out demons and worked many miracles." But I will tell them, "I will have nothing to do with you! Get out of my sight, you evil people!"

Two Builders

Anyone who hears and obeys these teachings of mine is like a wise person who built a house on solid rock. Rain poured down, rivers flooded, and winds beat against that house. But it did not fall, because it was built on solid rock.

Anyone who hears my teachings and does not obey them is like a foolish person who built a house on sand. The rain poured down, the rivers flooded, and the winds blew and beat against that house. Finally, it fell with a crash.

When Jesus finished speaking, the crowds were surprised at his teaching. He taught them like someone with authority, and not like their teachers of the Law of Moses.

Jesus Heals an Army Officer's Servant
(Luke 7.1-10)

After Jesus had finished teaching the people, he went to Capernaum. In that town an army officer's servant was sick and about to die. The officer liked this servant very much. And when he heard about Jesus, he sent some Jewish leaders to ask him to come and heal the servant.

The leaders went to Jesus and begged him to do something. They said, "This man deserves your help! He loves our nation and even built us a meeting place." So Jesus went with them.

When Jesus was not far from the house, the officer sent some friends to tell him, "Lord, don't go to any trouble for me! I am not good enough for you to come into my house. And I am certainly not worthy to come to you. Just say the word, and my servant will get well. I have officers who give orders to me, and I have soldiers who take orders from me. I can say to one of them, 'Go!' and he goes. I can say to another, 'Come!' and he comes. I can say to my servant, 'Do this!' and he will do it."

When Jesus heard this, he was so surprised that he turned and said to the crowd following him, "In all of Israel I've never found anyone with this much faith!"

The officer's friends returned and found the servant well.

A Widow's Son
(Luke 7.11-17)

Soon Jesus and his disciples were on their way to the town of Nain, and a big crowd was going along with them. As they came near the gate of the town, they saw people carrying out the body of a widow's only son. Many people from the town were walking along with her.

When the Lord saw the woman, he felt sorry for her and said, "Don't cry!"

Jesus went over and touched the stretcher on which the people were carrying the dead boy. They stopped, and Jesus said, "Young man, get up!" The boy sat up and began to speak. Jesus then gave him back to his mother.

Everyone was frightened and praised God. They said, "A great prophet is here with us! God has come to his people."

News about Jesus spread all over Judea and everywhere else in that part of the country.

We love Jesus when we know how much he has forgiven us.

Simon the Pharisee

(Luke 7.36-50)

A Pharisee invited Jesus to have dinner with him. So Jesus went to the Pharisee's home and got ready to eat.*

When a sinful woman in that town found out that Jesus was there, she bought an expensive bottle of perfume. Then she came and stood behind Jesus. She cried and started washing his feet with her tears and drying them with her hair. The woman kissed his feet and poured the perfume on them.

The Pharisee who had invited Jesus saw this and said to himself, "If this man really were a prophet, he would

know what kind of woman is touching him! He would know that she is a sinner."

Jesus said to the Pharisee, "Simon, I have something to say to you."

"Teacher, what is it?" Simon replied.

Jesus told him, "Two people were in debt to a moneylender. One of them owed him five hundred silver coins, and the other owed him fifty. Since neither of them could pay him back, the moneylender said that they didn't have to pay him anything. Which one of them will like him more?"

Simon answered, "I suppose it would be the one who had owed more and didn't have to pay it back."

"You are right," Jesus said.

He turned toward the woman and said to Simon, "Have you noticed this woman? When I came into your home, you didn't give me any water so I could wash my feet. But she has washed my feet with her tears and dried them with her hair. You didn't greet me with a kiss, but from the time I came in, she has not stopped kissing my feet. You didn't even pour olive oil on my head,* but she has poured expensive perfume on my feet. So I tell you that all her sins are forgiven, and that is why she has shown great love. But anyone who has been forgiven only a little will show only a little love."

Then Jesus said to the woman, "Your sins are forgiven."

Some other guests started saying to one another, "Who is this who dares to forgive sins?"

But Jesus told the woman, "Because of your faith, you are now saved.* May God give you peace!"

Jesus said we are in his family when we obey his Father. Then he told stories to show how we become members of his family.

Jesus' Mother and Brothers
(Mark 3.31-35)

Jesus' mother and brothers came and stood outside. Then they sent someone with a message for him to come out to them. The crowd that was sitting around Jesus told him, "Your mother and your brothers and sisters* are outside and want to see you."

Jesus asked, "Who is my mother and who are my brothers?" Then he looked at the people sitting around him and said, "Here are my mother and my brothers. Anyone who obeys God is my brother or sister or mother."

A Story about a Farmer
(Matthew 13.1-9)

That same day Jesus left the house and went out beside Lake Galilee, where he sat down to teach.* Such large crowds gathered around him that he had to sit in a boat, while the people stood on the shore. Then he taught them many things by using stories. He said:

A farmer went out to scatter seed in a field. While the farmer was scattering the seed, some of it fell along the road and was eaten by birds. Other seeds fell on thin, rocky ground and quickly started growing because the soil was not very deep. But when the sun came up, the plants were scorched and dried up, because they did not have enough roots. Some other seeds fell where thorn bushes grew up and choked the plants. But a few seeds did fall on good ground where the plants produced a hundred or sixty or thirty times as much as was scattered. If you have ears, pay attention!

Jesus Explains the Story about the Farmer
(Matthew 13.18-23)

Now listen to the meaning of the story about the farmer:

The seeds that fell along the road are the people who hear the message about the kingdom, but don't understand it. Then the evil one comes and snatches the message from their hearts. The seeds that fell on rocky ground are the people who gladly hear the message and accept it right away. But they don't have deep roots, and they don't last very long. As soon as life gets hard or the message gets them in trouble, they give up.

The seeds that fell among the thorn bushes are also people who hear the message. But they start worrying about the needs of this life and are fooled by the desire to get rich. So the message gets choked out, and they never produce anything. The seeds that fell on good ground are the people who hear and understand the message. They produce as much as a hundred or sixty or thirty times what was planted.

Weeds among the Wheat

(Matthew 13.24-30)

Jesus then told them this story:

The kingdom of heaven is like what happened when a farmer scattered good seed in a field. But while everyone was sleeping, an enemy came and scattered weed seeds in the field and then left.

When the plants came up and began to ripen, the farmer's servants could see the weeds. The servants came and asked, "Sir, didn't you scatter good seed in your field? Where did these weeds come from?"

"An enemy did this," he replied.

His servants then asked, "Do you want us to go out and pull up the weeds?"

"No!" he answered. "You might also pull up the wheat. Leave the weeds alone until harvest time. Then I'll tell my workers to gather the weeds and tie them up and burn them. But I'll have them store the wheat in my barn."

Jesus Explains the Story about the Weeds
(Matthew 13.36-43)

After Jesus left the crowd and went inside,* his disciples came to him and said, "Explain to us the story about the weeds in the wheat field."

Jesus answered:

> The one who scattered the good seed is the Son of Man. The field is the world, and the good seeds are the people who belong to the kingdom. The weed seeds are those who belong to the evil one, and the one who scattered them is the devil. The harvest is the end of time, and angels are the ones who bring in the harvest.
>
> Weeds are gathered and burned. That's how it will be at the end of time. The Son of Man will send out his angels, and they will gather from his kingdom everyone who does wrong or causes others to sin. Then he will throw them into a flaming furnace, where people will cry and grit their teeth in pain. But everyone who has done right will shine like the sun in their Father's kingdom. If you have ears, pay attention!

Then Jesus showed his disciples examples of how faith can work.

A Man with Evil Spirits
(Mark 5.1-20)

Jesus and his disciples crossed Lake Galilee and came to shore near the town of Gerasa.* When he was getting out of the boat, a man with an evil spirit quickly ran to him from the graveyard* where he had been living. No one was able to tie the man up anymore, not even with a chain.

He had often been put in chains and leg irons, but he broke the chains and smashed the leg irons. No one could control him. Night and day he was in the graveyard or on the hills, yelling and cutting himself with stones.

When the man saw Jesus in the distance, he ran up to him and kneeled down. He shouted, "Jesus, Son of God in heaven, what do you want with me? Promise me in God's name that you won't torture me!" The man said this because Jesus had already told the evil spirit to come out of him.

Jesus asked him, "What is your name?"

The man answered, "My name is Lots, because I have 'lots' of evil spirits." He then begged Jesus not to send them away.

Over on the hillside a large herd of pigs was feeding. So the evil spirits begged Jesus, "Send us into those pigs! Let us go into them." Jesus let them go, and they went out of the man and into the pigs. The whole herd of about two thousand pigs rushed down the steep bank into the lake and drowned.

The men taking care of the pigs ran to the town and the farms to spread the news. Then the people came out to see what had happened. When they came to Jesus, they saw the man who had once been full of demons. He was sitting there with his clothes on and in his right mind, and they were terrified.

Everyone who had seen what had happened told about the man and the pigs. Then the people started begging Jesus to leave their part of the country.

When Jesus was getting into the boat, the man begged to go with him. But Jesus would not let him. Instead, he said, "Go home to your family and tell them how much the Lord has done for you and how good he has been to you."

The man went away into the region near the ten cities known as Decapolis* and began telling everyone how much Jesus had done for him. Everyone who heard what happened was amazed.

A Dying Girl and a Sick Woman
(Mark 5.21-43)

Once again Jesus got into the boat and crossed Lake Galilee.* Then as he stood on the shore, a large crowd gathered around him. The person in charge of the Jewish meeting place was also there. His name was Jairus, and when he saw Jesus, he went over to him. He kneeled at Jesus' feet and started begging him for help. He said, "My daughter is about to die! Please come and touch her, so she will get well and live." Jesus went with Jairus. Many people followed along and kept crowding around.

In the crowd was a woman who had been bleeding for twelve years. She had gone to many doctors, and they had not done anything except cause her a lot of pain. She had paid them all the money she had. But instead of getting better, she only got worse.

The woman had heard about Jesus, so she came up behind him in the crowd and barely touched his clothes. She had said to herself, "If I can just touch his clothes, I will get well." As soon as she touched them, her bleeding stopped, and she knew she was well.

At that moment Jesus felt power go out from him. He turned to the crowd and asked, "Who touched my clothes?"

His disciples said to him, "Look at all these people crowding around you! How can you ask who touched you?" But Jesus turned to see who had touched him.

The woman knew what had happened to her. She came shaking with fear and kneeled down in front of Jesus. Then she told him the whole story.

Jesus said to the woman, "You are now well because of your faith. May God give you peace! You are healed, and you will no longer be in pain."

While Jesus was still speaking, some men came from Jairus' home and said, "Your daughter has died! Why bother the teacher anymore?"

Jesus heard* what they said, and he said to Jairus, "Don't worry. Just have faith!"

Jesus did not let anyone go with him except Peter and the two brothers, James and John. They went home with Jairus and saw the people crying and making a lot of noise.* Then Jesus went inside and said to them, "Why are you crying and carrying on like this? The child is not dead. She is just asleep." But the people laughed at him.

After Jesus had sent them all out of the house, he took the girl's father and mother and his three disciples and went to where she was. He took the twelve-year-old girl by the hand and said, "Talitha, koum!"* which means, "Little girl, get up!" The girl got right up and started walking around.

Everyone was greatly surprised. But Jesus ordered them not to tell anyone what had happened. Then he said, "Give her something to eat."

Now that Jesus had shown the apostles how to do God's work, he sent them on their first mission for him.

Instructions for the Twelve Apostles
(Luke 9.1-6)

Jesus called together his twelve apostles and gave them complete power over all demons and diseases. Then he sent them to tell about God's kingdom and to heal the sick. He told them, "Don't take anything with you! Don't take a walking stick or a traveling bag or food or money or even a change of clothes. When you are welcomed into a home, stay there until you leave that town. If people won't welcome you, leave the town and shake the dust from your feet* as a warning to them."

The apostles left and went from village to village, telling the good news and healing people everywhere.

The Death of John the Baptist
(Matthew 14.1-12)

About this time Herod the ruler* heard the news about Jesus and told his officials, "This is John the Baptist! He has come back from death, and that's why he has the power to work these miracles."

Herod had earlier arrested John and had him chained and put in prison. He did this because John had told him, "It isn't right for you to take Herodias, the wife of your brother Philip." Herod wanted to kill John. But the people thought John was a prophet, and Herod was afraid of what they might do.

When Herod's birthday came, the daughter of Herodias danced for the guests. She pleased Herod so much that he swore to give her whatever she wanted. But the girl's mother told her to say, "Here on a platter I want the head of John the Baptist!"

The king was sorry for what he had said. But he did not want to break the promise he had made in front of his guests. So he ordered a guard to go to the prison and cut off John's head. It was taken on a platter to the girl, and she gave it to her mother. John's followers took his body and buried it. Then they told Jesus what had happened.

So John the Baptist was killed while the apostles were on their mission for Jesus.

Jesus Feeds Five Thousand

(Mark 6.30-44)

After the apostles returned to Jesus,* they told him everything they had done and taught. But so many people were coming and going that Jesus and the apostles did not even have a chance to eat. Then Jesus said, "Let's go to a place* where we can be alone and get some rest." They left in a boat for a place where they could be alone. But many people saw them leave and figured out where they were going. So people from every town ran on ahead and got there first.

When Jesus got out of the boat, he saw the large crowd that was like sheep without a shepherd. He felt sorry for the people and started teaching them many things.

That evening the disciples came to Jesus and said, "This place is like a desert, and it is already late. Let the crowds leave, so they can go to the farms and villages near here and buy something to eat."

Jesus replied, "You give them something to eat."

But they asked him, "Don't you know that it would take almost a year's wages* to buy all of these people something to eat?"

Then Jesus said, "How much bread do you have? Go and see!"

They found out and answered, "We have five small loaves of bread* and two fish." Jesus told his disciples to have the people sit down on the green grass. They sat down in groups of a hundred and groups of fifty.

Jesus took the five loaves and the two fish. He looked up toward heaven and blessed the food. Then he broke the bread and handed it to his disciples to give to the people. He also divided the two fish, so that everyone could have some.

After everyone had eaten all they wanted, Jesus' disciples picked up twelve large baskets of leftover bread and fish.

There were five thousand men who ate the food.

Jesus Walks on the Water
(Matthew 14.22-33)

Right away Jesus made his disciples get into a boat and start back across the lake.* But he stayed until he had sent the crowds away. Then he went up on a mountain where he could be alone and pray. Later that evening, he was still there.

By this time the boat was a long way from the shore. It was going against the wind and was being tossed around

by the waves. A little while before morning, Jesus came walking on the water toward his disciples. When they saw him, they thought he was a ghost. They were terrified and started screaming.

At once Jesus said to them, "Don't worry! I am Jesus. Don't be afraid."

Peter replied, "Lord, if it is really you, tell me to come to you on the water."

"Come on!" Jesus said. Peter then got out of the boat and started walking on the water toward him.

But when Peter saw how strong the wind was, he was afraid and started sinking. "Lord, save me!" he shouted.

Right away Jesus reached out his hand. He helped Peter up and said, "You surely don't have much faith. Why do you doubt?"

When Jesus and Peter got into the boat, the wind died down. The men in the boat worshiped Jesus and said, "You really are the Son of God!"

The Bread That Gives Life
(John 6.22-59)

The people who had stayed on the east side of the lake knew that only one boat had been there. They also knew that Jesus had not left in it with his disciples. But the next day some boats from Tiberias sailed near the place where the crowd had eaten the bread for which the Lord had given thanks. They saw that Jesus and his disciples had left. Then they got into the boats and went to Capernaum to look for Jesus. They found him on the west side of the lake and asked, "Rabbi, when did you get here?"

Jesus answered, "I tell you for certain that you are not looking for me because you saw the miracles,* but because you ate all the food you wanted. Don't work for food that spoils. Work for food that gives eternal life. The Son of Man will give you this food, because God the Father has given him the right to do so."

"What exactly does God want us to do?" the people asked.

Jesus answered, "God wants you to have faith in the one he sent."

They replied, "What miracle will you work, so that we can have faith in you? What will you do? For example, when our ancestors were in the desert, they were given manna* to eat. It happened just as the Scriptures say, 'God gave them bread from heaven to eat.'"

Jesus then told them, "I tell you for certain that Moses was not the one who gave you bread from heaven. My Father is the one who gives you the true bread from heaven. And the bread that God gives is the one who came down from heaven to give life to the world."

The people said, "Lord, give us this bread and don't ever stop!"

Jesus replied:

I am the bread that gives life! No one who comes to me will ever be hungry. No one who has faith in me will ever be thirsty. I have told you already that you have seen me and still do not have faith in me. Everything and everyone that the Father has given me will come to me, and I won't turn any of them away.

I didn't come from heaven to do what I want! I came to do what the Father wants me to do. He sent me, and he wants to make certain that none of the ones he has given me will be lost. Instead, he wants me to raise them to life on the last day.* My Father wants everyone who sees the Son to have faith in him and to have eternal life. Then I will raise them to life on the last day.

The people started grumbling because Jesus had said he was the bread that had come down from heaven. They were asking each other, "Isn't he Jesus, the son of Joseph? Don't we know his father and mother? How can he say that he has come down from heaven?"

Jesus told them:

Stop grumbling! No one can come to me, unless the Father who sent me makes them want to come. But if they do come, I will raise them to life on the last day. One of the prophets wrote, "God will teach all of them." And so everyone who listens to the Father and learns from him will come to me.

The only one who has seen the Father is the one who has come from him. No one else has ever seen the Father. I tell you for certain that everyone who has faith in me has eternal life.

I am the bread that gives life! Your ancestors ate manna* in the desert, and later they died. But the bread from heaven has come down, so that no one who eats it will ever die. I am that bread from heaven! Everyone who eats it will live forever. My flesh is the life-giving bread that I give to the people of this world.

They started arguing with each other and asked, "How can he give us his flesh to eat?"

Jesus answered:

I tell you for certain that you won't live unless
you eat the flesh and drink the blood of the Son of
Man. But if you do eat my flesh and drink my blood,
you will have eternal life, and I will raise you to life
on the last day. My flesh is the true food, and my
blood is the true drink. If you eat my flesh and drink
my blood, you are one with me, and I am one with
you.

The living Father sent me, and I have life
because of him. Now everyone who eats my flesh will
live because of me. The bread that comes down from
heaven is not like what your ancestors ate. They died,
but whoever eats this bread will live forever.

Jesus was teaching in a Jewish place of worship in
Capernaum when he said these things.

*After the death of John the Baptist, Jesus was becoming
unpopular in his own country. So he decided to serve in a
new area for a while.*

A Woman's Faith
(Matthew 15.21-28)

Jesus left and went to the territory near the cities of
Tyre and Sidon. Suddenly a Canaanite woman* from there
came out shouting, "Lord and Son of David,* have pity on
me! My daughter is full of demons." Jesus did not say a
word. But the woman kept following along and shouting,
so his disciples came up and asked him to send her away.

Jesus said, "I was sent only to the people of Israel!
They are like a flock of lost sheep."

The woman came closer. Then she kneeled down and begged, "Lord, please help me!"

Jesus replied, "It isn't right to take food away from children and feed it to dogs."*

"Lord, that's true," the woman said, "but even dogs get the crumbs that fall from their owner's table."

Jesus answered, "Dear woman, you really do have a lot of faith, and you will be given what you want." At that moment her daughter was healed.

The country where Jesus healed the woman's daughter was Phoenicia, a nation on the northern border of Palestine. Then he crossed back into Palestine and came to the city of Caesarea Philippi.

Who Is Jesus?
(Matthew 16.13-20)

When Jesus and his disciples were near the town of Caesarea Philippi, he asked them, "What do people say about the Son of Man?"

The disciples answered, "Some people say you are John the Baptist or maybe Elijah* or Jeremiah or some other prophet."

Then Jesus asked them, "But who do you say I am?"

Simon Peter spoke up, "You are the Messiah, the Son of the living God."

Jesus told him:

Simon, son of Jonah, you are blessed! You didn't discover this on your own. It was shown to you by my Father in heaven. So I will call you Peter, which

means "a rock." On this rock I will build my church, and death itself will not have any power over it. I will give you the keys to the kingdom of heaven, and God in heaven will allow whatever you allow on earth. But he will not allow anything that you don't allow.

Jesus told his disciples not to tell anyone that he was the Messiah.

The True Glory of Jesus

(Matthew 17.1-13)

Six days later Jesus took Peter and the brothers James and John with him. They went up on a very high mountain where they could be alone. There in front of the disciples Jesus was completely changed. His face was shining like the sun, and his clothes became white as light.

All at once Moses and Elijah were there talking with Jesus. So Peter said to him, "Lord, it is good for us to be here! Let us make three shelters, one for you, one for Moses, and one for Elijah."

While Peter was still speaking, the shadow of a bright cloud passed over them. From the cloud a voice said, "This is my own dear Son, and I am pleased with him. Listen to what he says!" When the disciples heard the voice, they were so afraid that they fell flat on the ground. But Jesus came over and touched them. He said, "Get up and don't be afraid!" When they opened their eyes, they saw only Jesus.

On their way down from the mountain, Jesus warned his disciples not to tell anyone what they had seen until after the Son of Man had been raised from death.

The disciples asked Jesus, "Don't the teachers of the Law of Moses say that Elijah must come before the Messiah does?"

Jesus told them, "Elijah certainly will come and get everything ready. In fact, he has already come. But the people did not recognize him and treated him just as they wanted to. They will soon make the Son of Man suffer in the same way." Then the disciples understood that Jesus was talking to them about John the Baptist.

Jesus' Brothers Don't Have Faith in Him

(John 7.2-9)

It was almost time for the Festival of Shelters, and Jesus' brothers said to him, "Why don't you go to Judea? Then your disciples can see what you are doing. No one does anything in secret, if they want others to know about them. So let the world know what you are doing!" Even Jesus' own brothers had not yet become his followers.

Jesus answered, "My time hasn't yet come,* but your time is always here. The people of this world cannot hate you. They hate me, because I tell them that they do evil things. Go on to the festival. My time hasn't yet come, and I am not going." Jesus said this and stayed on in Galilee.

Jesus at the Festival of Shelters

(John 7.10-31)

After Jesus' brothers had gone to the festival, he decided to go, and he went secretly, without telling anyone.

During the festival the Jewish leaders looked for Jesus and asked, "Where is he?" The crowds even got into an argument about him. Some were saying, "Jesus is a good man," while others were saying, "He is lying to everyone." But the people were afraid of their leaders, and none of them talked in public about him.

When the festival was about half over, Jesus stood up and started teaching in the temple. The leaders were surprised and said, "How does this man know so much? He has never been taught!"

Jesus replied:

I am not teaching something that I thought up. What I teach comes from the one who sent me. If you really want to obey God, you will know if what I teach comes from God or from me. If I wanted to bring honor to myself, I would speak for myself. But I want to honor the one who sent me. That is why I tell the truth and not a lie. Didn't Moses give you the Law? Yet none of you obey it! So why do you want to kill me?

The crowd replied, "You're crazy! What makes you think someone wants to kill you?"

Jesus answered:

I worked one miracle,* and it amazed you. Moses commanded you to circumcise your sons. But it wasn't really Moses who gave you this command. It was your ancestors, and even on the Sabbath you circumcise your sons in order to obey the Law of Moses. Why are you angry with me for making someone completely well on the Sabbath? Don't judge by appearances. Judge by what is right.

Some of the people from Jerusalem were saying, "Isn't this the man they want to kill? Yet here he is, speaking for everyone to hear. And no one is arguing with him. Do you suppose the authorities know that he is the Messiah? But how could that be? No one knows where the Messiah will come from, but we know where this man comes from."

As Jesus was teaching in the temple, he shouted, "Do you really think you know me and where I came from? I didn't come on my own! The one who sent me is truthful, and you don't know him. But I know the one who sent me, because I came from him."

Some of the people wanted to arrest Jesus right then. But no one even laid a hand on him, because his time had not yet come.* A lot of people in the crowd put their faith in him and said, "When the Messiah comes, he surely won't perform more miracles* than this man has done!"

Streams of Life-Giving Water
(John 7.37-39)

On the last and most important day of the festival, Jesus stood up and shouted, "If you are thirsty, come to me and drink! Have faith in me, and you will have life-giving water flowing from deep inside you, just as the Scriptures say." Jesus was talking about the Holy Spirit, who would be given to everyone that had faith in him. The Spirit had not yet been given to anyone, since Jesus had not yet been given his full glory.*

A Woman Caught in Sin

(John 7.53—8.11)

Everyone else went home, but Jesus walked out to the Mount of Olives. Then early the next morning he went to the temple. The people came to him, and he sat down* and started teaching them.

The Pharisees and the teachers of the Law of Moses brought in a woman who had been caught in bed with a man who was not her husband. They made her stand in the middle of the crowd. Then they said, "Teacher, this woman was caught sleeping with a man who is not her husband. The Law of Moses teaches that a woman like this should be stoned to death! What do you say?"

They asked Jesus this question, because they wanted to test him and bring some charge against him. But Jesus simply bent over and started writing on the ground with his finger.

They kept on asking Jesus about the woman. Finally, he stood up and said, "If any of you have never sinned, then go ahead and throw the first stone at her!" Once again he bent over and began writing on the ground. The people left one by one, beginning with the oldest one in the crowd. Finally, Jesus and the woman were there alone.

Jesus stood up and asked her, "Where is everyone? Isn't there anyone left to accuse you?"

"No sir," the woman answered.

Then Jesus told her, "I am not going to accuse you either. You may go now, but don't sin anymore."*

Jesus Heals a Man Born Blind

(John 9.1-41)

As Jesus walked along, he saw a man who had been blind since birth. Jesus' disciples asked, "Teacher, why was this man born blind? Was it because he or his parents sinned?"

"No, it wasn't!" Jesus answered. "But because of this, you will see God work a miracle for him. As long as it is day, we must do what the one who sent me wants me to

do. When night comes, no one can work. While I am in the world, I am the light for the world."

After Jesus said this, he spit on the ground. He made some mud and smeared it on the man's eyes. Then he said, "Go and wash off the mud in Siloam Pool." The man went and washed in Siloam, which means "One Who Is Sent." When he had washed off the mud, he could see.

The man's neighbors and the people who had seen him begging wondered if he really could be the same man. Some of them said he was the same beggar, while others said he only looked like him. But he told them, "I am that man."

"Then how can you see?" they asked.

He answered, "Someone named Jesus made some mud and smeared it on my eyes. He told me to go and wash it off in Siloam Pool. When I did, I could see."

"Where is he now?" they asked.

"I don't know," he answered.

The Pharisees Try to Find Out What Happened

The day when Jesus made the mud and healed the man was a Sabbath. So the people took the man to the Pharisees. They asked him how he was able to see, and he answered, "Jesus made some mud and smeared it on my eyes. Then after I washed off the mud, I could see."

Some of the Pharisees said, "This man Jesus does not come from God. If he did, he would not break the law of the Sabbath."

Others asked, "How could someone who is a sinner work such a miracle?"*

Since the Pharisees could not agree among themselves,

they asked the man, "What do you say about this one who healed your eyes?"

"He is a prophet!" the man told them.

But the Jewish leaders would not believe that the man had once been blind. They sent for his parents and asked them, "Is this the son that you said was born blind? How can he now see?"

The man's parents answered, "We are certain that he is our son, and we know that he was born blind. But we don't know how he got his sight or who gave it to him. Ask him! He is old enough to speak for himself."

The man's parents said this because they were afraid of the Jewish leaders. The leaders had already agreed that no one was to have anything to do with anyone who said Jesus was the Messiah.

The leaders called the man back and said, "Swear by God to tell the truth! We know that Jesus is a sinner."

The man replied, "I don't know if he is a sinner or not. All I know is that I used to be blind, but now I can see!"

"What did he do to you?" the Jewish leaders asked. "How did he heal your eyes?"

The man answered, "I have already told you once, and you refused to listen. Why do you want me to tell you again? Do you also want to become his disciples?"

The leaders insulted the man and said, "You are his follower! We are followers of Moses. We are sure that God spoke to Moses, but we don't even know where Jesus comes from."

The man replied, "How strange! He healed my eyes, and yet you don't know where he comes from. We know that God listens only to people who love and obey him. God doesn't listen to sinners. And this is the first time in history that anyone has ever given sight to someone born blind. Jesus could not do anything unless he came from God."

The leaders told the man, "You have been a sinner since the day you were born! Do you think you can teach us anything?" Then they said, "You can never come back into any of our meeting places!"

When Jesus heard what had happened, he went and found the man. Then Jesus asked, "Do you have faith in the Son of Man?"

He replied, "Sir, if you will tell me who he is, I will put my faith in him."

"You have already seen him," Jesus answered, "and right now he is talking with you."

The man said, "Lord, I put my faith in you!" Then he worshiped Jesus.

Jesus told him, "I came to judge the people of this world. I am here to give sight to the blind and to make blind everyone who sees."

When the Pharisees heard Jesus say this, they asked, "Are we blind?"

Jesus answered, "If you were blind, you would not be guilty. But now that you claim to see, you will keep on being guilty."

A Story about Sheep

(John 10.1-6)

Jesus said:

I tell you for certain that only thieves and robbers climb over the fence instead of going in through the gate to the sheep pen. But the gatekeeper opens the gate for the shepherd, and he goes in through it. The sheep know their shepherd's voice. He calls each of them by name and leads them out.

When he has led out all of his sheep, he walks in front of them, and they follow, because they know his voice. The sheep will not follow strangers. They don't recognize a stranger's voice, and they run away.

Jesus told the people this story. But they did not understand what he was talking about.

Jesus Is the Good Shepherd
(John 10.7-21)

Jesus said:

I tell you for certain that I am the gate for the sheep. Everyone who came before me was a thief or a robber, and the sheep did not listen to any of them. I am the gate. All who come in through me will be saved. Through me they will come and go and find pasture.

A thief comes only to rob, kill, and destroy. I came so that everyone would have life, and have it in its fullest. I am the good shepherd, and the good shepherd gives up his life for his sheep. Hired workers are not like the shepherd. They don't own the sheep, and when they see a wolf coming, they run off and leave the sheep. Then the wolf attacks and scatters the flock. Hired workers run away because they don't care about the sheep.

I am the good shepherd. I know my sheep, and they know me. Just as the Father knows me, I know the Father, and I give up my life for my sheep. I have

other sheep that are not in this sheep pen. I must
bring them together too, when they hear my voice.
Then there will be one flock of sheep and one shepherd.

The Father loves me, because I give up my life,
so that I may receive it back again. No one takes my
life from me. I give it up willingly! I have the power
to give it up and the power to receive it back again,
just as my Father commanded me to do.

The Jews took sides because of what Jesus had told
them. Many of them said, "He has a demon in him! He is
crazy! Why listen to him?"

But others said, "How could anyone with a demon in

him say these things? No one like that could give sight to a blind person!"

The Good Samaritan
(Luke 10.25-37)

An expert in the Law of Moses stood up and asked Jesus a question to see what he would say. "Teacher," he asked, "What must I do to have eternal life?"

Jesus answered, "What is written in the Scriptures? How do you understand them?"

The man replied, "The Scriptures say, 'Love the Lord your God with all your heart, soul, strength, and mind.' They also say, 'Love your neighbors as much as you love yourself.'"

Jesus said, "You have given the right answer. If you do this, you will have eternal life."

But the man wanted to show that he knew what he was talking about. So he asked Jesus, "Who are my neighbors?"

Jesus replied:

As a man was going down from Jerusalem to Jericho, robbers attacked him and grabbed everything

he had. They beat him up and ran off, leaving him half dead.

A priest happened to be going down the same road. But when he saw the man, he walked by on the other side. Later a temple helper* came to the same place. But when he saw the man who had been beaten up, he also went by on the other side.

A man from Samaria then came traveling along that road. When he saw the man, he felt sorry for him and went over to him. He treated his wounds with olive oil and wine* and bandaged them. Then he put him on his own donkey and took him to an inn, where he took care of him. The next morning he gave the innkeeper two silver coins and said, "Please take care of the man. If you spend more than this on him, I will pay you when I return."

Then Jesus asked, "Which one of these three people was a real neighbor to the man who was beaten up by robbers?"

The teacher answered, "The one who showed pity."

Jesus said, "Go and do the same!"

Martha and Mary

(Luke 10.38-42)

The Lord and his disciples were traveling along and
came to a village. When they got there, a woman named
Martha welcomed him into her home. She had a sister named
Mary, who sat down in front of the Lord and was listening

to what he said. Martha was worried about all that had to be done. Finally, she went to Jesus and said, "Lord, doesn't it bother you that my sister has left me to do all the work by myself? Tell her to come and help me!"

The Lord answered, "Martha, Martha! You are worried and upset about so many things, but only one thing is necessary. Mary has chosen what is best, and it will not be taken away from her."

A Rich Fool

(Luke 12.13-21)

A man in a crowd said to Jesus, "Teacher, tell my brother to give me my share of what our father left us when he died."

Jesus answered, "Who gave me the right to settle arguments between you and your brother?"

Then he said to the crowd, "Don't be greedy! Owning a lot of things won't make your life safe."

So Jesus told them this story:

A rich man's farm produced a big crop, and he said to himself, "What can I do? I don't have a place large enough to store everything."

Later, he said, "Now I know what I'll do. I'll tear down my barns and build bigger ones, where I can store all my grain and other goods. Then I'll say to myself, 'You have stored up enough good things to last for years to come. Live it up! Eat, drink, and enjoy yourself.'"

But God said to him, "You fool! Tonight you will die. Then who will get what you have stored up?"

"This is what happens to people who store up everything for themselves, but are poor in the sight of God."

Healing a Woman on the Sabbath

(Luke 13.10-17)

One Sabbath Jesus was teaching in a Jewish meeting place, and a woman was there who had been crippled by an evil spirit for eighteen years. She was completely bent over and could not straighten up. When Jesus saw the woman, he called her over and said, "You are now well." He placed his hands on her, and right away she stood up straight and praised God.

The man in charge of the meeting place was angry because Jesus had healed someone on the Sabbath. So he said to the people, "Each week has six days when we can work. Come and be healed on one of those days, but not on the Sabbath."

The Lord replied, "Are you trying to fool someone? Won't any one of you untie your ox or donkey and lead it out to drink on a Sabbath? This woman belongs to the family of Abraham, but Satan has kept her bound for eighteen years. Isn't it right to set her free on the Sabbath?" Jesus' words made all his enemies ashamed. But everyone else in the crowd was happy about the wonderful things he was doing.

Being a Disciple
(Luke 14.25-33)

Large crowds were walking along with Jesus, when he turned and said:

You cannot be my disciple, unless you love me more than you love your father and mother, your wife and children, and your brothers and sisters. You cannot come with me unless you love me more than you love your own life.

You cannot be my disciple unless you carry your own cross and come with me.

Suppose one of you wants to build a tower. What is the first thing you will do? Won't you sit down and figure out how much it will cost and if you have enough money to pay for it? Otherwise, you will start building the tower, but not be able to finish. Then everyone who sees what is happening will laugh at you. They will say, "You started building, but could not finish the job."

What will a king do if he has only ten thousand soldiers to defend himself against a king who is about to attack him with twenty thousand soldiers? Before he goes out to battle, won't he first sit down and decide if he can win? If he thinks he won't be able to defend himself, he will send messengers and ask for peace while the other king is still a long way off. So then, you cannot be my disciple unless you give away everything you own.

One Sheep
(Luke 15.1-7)

Tax collectors* and sinners were all crowding around to listen to Jesus. So the Pharisees and the teachers of the Law of Moses started grumbling, "This man is friendly with sinners. He even eats with them."

Then Jesus told them this story:

> If any of you has a hundred sheep, and one of them gets lost, what will you do? Won't you leave the ninety-nine in the field and go look for the lost sheep until you find it? And when you find it, you will be so glad that you will put it on your shoulder and carry it home. Then you will call in your friends and neighbors and say, "Let's celebrate! I've found my lost sheep."

Jesus said, "In the same way there is more happiness in heaven because of one sinner who turns to God than over ninety-nine good people who don't need to."

One Coin
(Luke 15.8-10)

Jesus told the people another story:

What will a woman do if she has ten silver coins and loses one of them? Won't she light a lamp, sweep the floor, and look carefully until she finds it? Then she will call in her friends and neighbors and say, "Let's celebrate! I've found the coin I lost."

Jesus said, "In the same way God's angels are happy when even one person turns to him."

Two Sons
(Luke 15.11-32)

Jesus also told them another story:

Once a man had two sons. The younger son said to his father, "Give me my share of the property." So the father divided his property between his two sons.

Not long after that, the younger son packed up everything he owned and left for a foreign country, where he wasted all his money in wild living. He had spent everything, when a bad famine spread through that whole land. Soon he had nothing to eat.

He went to work for a man in that country, and the man sent him out to take care of his pigs.* He would have been glad to eat what the pigs were eating,* but no one gave him a thing.

Finally, he came to his senses and said, "My father's workers have plenty to eat, and here I am, starving to death! I will leave and go to my father and say to him, 'Father, I have sinned against God in heaven and against you. I am no longer good enough to be called your son. Treat me like one of your workers.' "

The younger son got up and started back to his
father. But when he was still a long way off, his father
saw him and felt sorry for him. He ran to his son
and hugged and kissed him.

The son said, "Father, I have sinned against
God in heaven and against you. I am no longer good
enough to be called your son."

But his father said to the servants, "Hurry and
bring the best clothes and put them on him. Give him
a ring for his finger and sandals* for his feet. Get
the best calf and prepare it, so we can eat and celebrate.
This son of mine was dead, but has now come back
to life. He was lost and has now been found." And
they began to celebrate.

The older son had been out in the field. But when he came near the house, he heard the music and dancing. So he called one of the servants over and asked, "What's going on here?"

The servant answered, "Your brother has come home safe and sound, and your father ordered us to kill the best calf." The older brother got so mad that he would not even go into the house.

His father came out and begged him to go in. But he said to his father, "For years I have worked for you like a slave and have always obeyed you. But you have never even given me a little goat, so that I could give a dinner for my friends. This other son of yours wasted your money on bad women. And now that he has come home, you ordered the best calf to be killed for a feast."

His father replied, "My son, you are always with me, and everything I have is yours. But we should be glad and celebrate! Your brother was dead, but he is now alive. He was lost and has now been found."

Lazarus and the Rich Man
(Luke 16.19-31)

There was once a rich man who wore expensive clothes and every day ate the best food. But a poor beggar named Lazarus was brought to the gate of the rich man's house. He was happy just to eat the scraps that fell from the rich man's table. His body was covered with sores, and dogs kept coming up to lick them. The poor man died, and angels took him to the place of honor next to Abraham.*

The rich man also died and was buried. He went to hell* and was suffering terribly. When he looked

up and saw Abraham far off and Lazarus at his side, he said to Abraham, "Have pity on me! Send Lazarus to dip his finger in water and touch my tongue. I'm suffering terribly in this fire."

Abraham answered, "My friend, remember that while you lived, you had everything good, and Lazarus had everything bad. Now he is happy, and you are in pain. And besides, there is a deep ditch between us, and no one from either side can cross over."

But the rich man said, "Abraham, then please send Lazarus to my father's home. Let him warn my five brothers, so they won't come to this horrible place."

Abraham answered, "Your brothers can read what Moses and the prophets* wrote. They should pay attention to that."

Then the rich man said, "No, that's not enough! If only someone from the dead would go to them, they would listen and turn to God."

So Abraham said, "If they won't pay attention

to Moses and the prophets, they won't listen even to someone who comes back from the dead."

The Death of Lazarus
(John 11.1-16)

A man by the name of Lazarus was sick in the village of Bethany. He had two sisters, Mary and Martha. This was the same Mary who later poured perfume on the Lord's head and wiped his feet with her hair. The sisters sent a message to the Lord and told him that his good friend Lazarus was sick.

When Jesus heard this, he said, "His sickness won't end in death. It will bring glory to God and his Son."

Jesus loved Martha and her sister and brother. But he stayed where he was for two more days. Then he said to his disciples, "Now we'll go back to Judea."

"Teacher," they said, "the people there want to stone you to death! Why do you want to go back?"

Jesus answered, "Aren't there twelve hours in each day? If you walk during the day, you will have light from the sun, and you won't stumble. But if you walk during the night, you will stumble, because there isn't any light inside you." Then he told them, "Our friend Lazarus is asleep, and I am going there to wake him up."

They replied, "Lord, if he is asleep, he will get better." Jesus really meant that Lazarus was dead, but they thought he was talking only about sleep.

Then Jesus told them plainly, "Lazarus is dead! I am glad that I wasn't there, because now you will have a chance to put your faith in me. Let's go to him."

Thomas, whose nickname was "Twin," said to the other disciples, "Come on. Let's go so we can die with him."

Jesus Brings Lazarus to Life

(John 11.17-44)

When Jesus got to Bethany, he found that Lazarus had already been in the tomb four days. Bethany was only about two miles from Jerusalem, and many people had come from the city to comfort Martha and Mary because their brother had died.

When Martha heard that Jesus had arrived, she went out to meet him, but Mary stayed in the house. Martha said to Jesus, "Lord, if you had been here, my brother would not have died. Yet even now I know that God will do anything you ask."

Jesus told her, "Your brother will live again!"

Martha answered, "I know that he will be raised to life on the last day,* when all the dead are raised."

Jesus then said, "I am the one who raises the dead to life! Everyone who has faith in me will live, even if they die. And everyone who lives because of faith in me will never die. Do you believe this?"

"Yes, Lord!" she replied. "I believe that you are Christ, the Son of God. You are the one we hoped would come into the world."

After Martha said this, she went and privately said to her sister Mary, "The Teacher is here, and he wants to see you." As soon as Mary heard this, she got up and went out to Jesus. He was still outside the village where Martha had gone to meet him. Many people had come to comfort Mary, and when they saw her quickly leave the house, they thought she was going out to the tomb to cry. So they followed her.

Mary went to where Jesus was. Then as soon as she saw him, she kneeled at his feet and said, "Lord, if you had been here, my brother would not have died."

When Jesus saw that Mary and the people with her were crying, he was terribly upset and asked, "Where have you put his body?"

They replied, "Lord, come and you will see."

Jesus started crying, and the people said, "See how much he loved Lazarus."

Some of them said, "He gives sight to the blind. Why couldn't he have kept Lazarus from dying?"

Jesus was still terribly upset. So he went to the tomb, which was a cave with a stone rolled against the entrance. Then he told the people to roll the stone away. But Martha said, "Lord, you know that Lazarus has been dead four days, and there will be a bad smell."

Jesus replied, "Didn't I tell you that if you had faith, you would see the glory of God?"

After the stone had been rolled aside, Jesus looked up toward heaven and prayed, "Father, I thank you for answering my prayer. I know that you always answer my prayers. But I said this, so that the people here would believe that you sent me."

When Jesus had finished praying, he shouted, "Lazarus, come out!" The man who had been dead came out. His hands and feet were wrapped with strips of burial cloth, and a cloth covered his face.

Jesus then told the people, "Untie him and let him go."

Jesus was now on the way to his last Passover festival in Jerusalem.

Ten Men with Leprosy
(Luke 17.11-19)

On his way to Jerusalem, Jesus went along the border between Samaria and Galilee. As he was going into a village, ten men with leprosy* came toward him. They stood at a distance and shouted, "Jesus, Master, have pity on us!"

Jesus looked at them and said, "Go show yourselves to the priests."*

On their way they were healed. When one of them discovered that he was healed, he came back, shouting praises to God. He bowed down at the feet of Jesus and thanked him. The man was from the country of Samaria.

Jesus asked, "Weren't ten men healed? Where are the other nine? Why was this foreigner the only one who came back to thank God?" Then Jesus told the man, "You may get up and go. Your faith has made you well."

A Widow and a Judge
(Luke 18.1-8)

Jesus told his disciples a story about how they should keep on praying and never give up:

In a town there was once a judge who didn't fear God or care about people. In that same town there was a widow who kept going to the judge and saying, "Make sure that I get fair treatment in court."

For a while the judge refused to do anything. Finally, he said to himself, "Even though I don't fear God or care about people, I will help this widow because she keeps on bothering me. If I don't help her, she will wear me out."

The Lord said:

Think about what that crooked judge said. Won't God protect his chosen ones who pray to him day and night? Won't he be concerned for them? He will surely hurry and help them. But when the Son of Man comes, will he find on this earth anyone with faith?

A Pharisee and a Tax Collector

(Luke 18.9-14)

Jesus told a story to some people who thought they were better than others and who looked down on everyone else:

Two men went into the temple to pray.* One was a Pharisee and the other a tax collector.* The Pharisee stood over by himself and prayed,* "God, I thank you that I am not greedy, dishonest, and unfaithful in marriage like other people. And I am really glad that I am not like that tax collector over there. I go without eating* for two days a week, and I give you one tenth of all I earn."

The tax collector stood off at a distance and did not think he was good enough even to look up toward heaven. He was so sorry for what he had done that he pounded his chest and prayed, "God, have pity on me! I am such a sinner."

Then Jesus said, "When the two men went home, it was the tax collector and not the Pharisee who was pleasing to God. If you put yourself above others, you will be put down. But if you humble yourself, you will be honored."

Jesus Blesses Little Children

(Mark 10.13-16)

Some people brought their children to Jesus so that he could bless them by placing his hands on them. But his disciples told the people to stop bothering him.

When Jesus saw this, he became angry and said, "Let the children come to me! Don't try to stop them. People who are like these little children belong to the kingdom of God.* I promise you that you cannot get into God's kingdom, unless you accept it the way a child does." Then Jesus took the

children in his arms and blessed them by placing his hands
on them.

Workers in a Vineyard
(Matthew 20.1-16)

As Jesus was telling what the kingdom of heaven would
be like, he said:

Early one morning a man went out to hire some
workers for his vineyard. After he had agreed to pay

them the usual amount for a day's work, he sent them off to his vineyard.

About nine that morning, the man saw some other people standing in the market with nothing to do. He said he would pay them what was fair, if they would work in his vineyard. So they went.

At noon and again about three in the afternoon he returned to the market. And each time he made the same agreement with others who were loafing around with nothing to do.

Finally, about five in the afternoon the man went back and found some others standing there. He asked them, "Why have you been standing here all day long doing nothing?"

"Because no one has hired us," they answered. Then he told them to go work in his vineyard.

That evening the owner of the vineyard told the man in charge of the workers to call them in and give them their money. He also told the man to begin with the ones who were hired last. When the workers arrived, the ones who had been hired at five in the afternoon were given a full day's pay.

The workers who had been hired first thought they would be given more than the others. But when they were given the same, they began complaining to the owner of the vineyard. They said, "The ones who were hired last worked for only one hour. But you paid them the same that you did us. And we worked in the hot sun all day long!"

The owner answered one of them, "Friend, I didn't cheat you. I paid you exactly what we agreed on. Take your money now and go! What business is it of yours if I want to pay them the same that I paid you? Don't I have the right to do what I want with my own money? Why should you be jealous, if I want to be generous?"

Jesus then said, "So it is. Everyone who is now first will be last, and everyone who is last will be first."

A Mother's Request
(Matthew 20.20-28)

The mother of James and John* came to Jesus with her two sons. She kneeled down and started begging him to do something for her. Jesus asked her what she wanted, and she said, "When you come into your kingdom, please let one of my sons sit at your right side and the other at your left."*

Jesus answered, "Not one of you knows what you are asking. Are you able to drink from the cup* that I must soon drink from?"

James and John said, "Yes, we are!"

Jesus replied, "You certainly will drink from my cup! But it is not for me to say who will sit at my right side and at my left. That is for my Father to say."

When the ten other disciples heard this, they were angry with the two brothers. But Jesus called the disciples together and said:

> You know that foreign rulers like to order their people around. And their great leaders have full power over everyone they rule. But don't act like them. If you want to be great, you must be the servant of all the others. And if you want to be first, you must be the slave of the rest. The Son of Man did not come to be a slave master, but a slave who will give his life to rescue* many people.

Zaccheus

(Luke 19.1-10)

Jesus was going through Jericho, where a man named Zaccheus lived. He was in charge of collecting taxes* and was very rich. Jesus was heading his way, and Zaccheus wanted to see what he was like. But Zaccheus was a short man and could not see over the crowd. So he ran ahead and climbed up into a sycamore tree.

When Jesus got there, he looked up and said, "Zaccheus, hurry down! I want to stay with you today." Zaccheus hurried down and gladly welcomed Jesus.

Everyone who saw this started grumbling, "This man Zaccheus is a sinner! And Jesus is going home to eat with him."

Later that day Zaccheus stood up and said to the Lord, "I will give half of my property to the poor. And I

will now pay back four times as much* to everyone I have ever cheated."

Jesus said to Zacchaeus, "Today you and your family have been saved,* because you are a true son of Abraham.* The Son of Man came to look for and to save people who are lost."

A Story about Ten Servants
(Luke 19.11-27)

The people were still listening to Jesus as he was getting close to Jerusalem. Many of them thought that God's kingdom would soon appear, and Jesus told them this story:

A prince once went to a foreign country to be crowned king and then to return. But before leaving, he called in ten servants and gave each of them some money. He told them, "Use this to earn more money until I get back."

But the people of his country hated him, and they sent messengers to the foreign country to say, "We don't want this man to be our king."

After the prince had been made king, he returned and called in his servants. He asked them how much they had earned with the money they had been given.

The first servant came and said, "Sir, with the money you gave me I have earned ten times as much."

"That's fine, my good servant!" the king said. "Since you have shown that you can be trusted with a small amount, you will be given ten cities to rule."

The second one came and said, "Sir, with the money you gave me, I have earned five times as much."

The king said, "You will be given five cities."

Another servant came and said, "Sir, here is your money. I kept it safe in a handkerchief. You are

a hard man, and I was afraid of you. You take what is not yours, and you harvest crops you didn't plant."

"You worthless servant!" the king told him. "You have condemned yourself by what you have just said. You knew that I am a hard man, taking what is not mine and harvesting what I've not planted. Why didn't you put my money in the bank? On my return, I could have had the money together with interest."

Then he said to some other servants standing there, "Take the money away from him and give it to the servant who earned ten times as much."

But they said, "Sir, he already has ten times as much!"

The king replied, "Those who have something will be given more. But everything will be taken away from those who don't have anything. Now bring me the enemies who didn't want me to be their king. Kill them while I watch!"

Jesus Enters Jerusalem

(Matthew 21.1-11)

When Jesus and his disciples came near to Jerusalem, he went to Bethphage on the Mount of Olives and sent two of them on ahead. He told them, "Go into the next village, where you will at once find a donkey and her colt. Untie the two donkeys and bring them to me. If anyone asks why you are doing that, just say, 'The Lord* needs them.' Right away he will let you have the donkeys."

So God's promise came true, just as the prophet had said,

"Announce to the people
of Jerusalem:
'Your king is coming to you!
He is humble
and rides on a donkey.
He comes on the colt
of a donkey.'"

The disciples left and did what Jesus had told them to do. They brought the donkey and its colt and laid some clothes on their backs. Then Jesus got on.

Many people spread clothes in the road, while others put down branches* which they had cut from trees. Some

people walked ahead of Jesus and others followed behind.
They were all shouting,

> "Hooray* for the Son of David!*
> God bless the one who comes
>   in the name of the Lord.
> Hooray for God
>   in heaven above!"

When Jesus came to Jerusalem, everyone in the city was excited and asked, "Who can this be?"

The crowd answered, "This is Jesus, the prophet from Nazareth in Galilee."

Paying Taxes

(Luke 20.20-26)

Jesus' enemies kept watching him closely, because they wanted to hand him over to the Roman governor. So they sent some men who pretended to be good. But they were really spies trying to catch Jesus saying something wrong. The spies said to him, "Teacher, we know that you teach the truth about what God wants people to do. And you treat everyone with the same respect, no matter who they are. Tell us, should we pay taxes to the Emperor or not?"

Jesus knew that they were trying to trick him. So he told them, "Show me a coin." Then he asked, "Whose picture and name are on it?"

"The Emperor's," they answered.

Then he told them, "Give the Emperor what belongs to him and give God what belongs to God." Jesus' enemies could not catch him saying anything wrong there in front of the people. They were amazed at his answer and kept quiet.

A Widow's Offering

(Luke 21.1-4)

Jesus looked up and saw some rich people tossing their gifts into the offering box. He also saw a poor widow putting in two pennies. And he said, "I tell you that this poor woman has put in more than all the others. Everyone else gave what they didn't need. But she is very poor and gave everything she had."

A Story about Ten Girls

(Matthew 25.1-13)

The kingdom of heaven is like what happened one night when ten girls took their oil lamps and went to a wedding to meet the groom.* Five of the girls were foolish and five were wise. The foolish ones took their lamps, but no extra oil. The ones who were wise took along extra oil for their lamps.

The groom was late arriving, and the girls became drowsy and fell asleep. Then in the middle of the night someone shouted, "Here's the groom! Come to meet him!"

When the girls got up and started getting their lamps ready, the foolish ones said to the others, "Let us have some of your oil! Our lamps are going out."

The girls who were wise answered, "There's not enough oil for all of us! Go and buy some for yourselves."

While the foolish girls were on their way to get some oil, the groom arrived. The girls who were ready went into the wedding, and the doors were closed. Later the other girls returned and shouted, "Sir, sir! Open the door for us!"

But the groom replied, "I don't even know you!"

So, my disciples, always be ready! You don't know the day or the time when all this will happen.

A Plot to Kill Jesus
(Luke 22.1-6)

The Feast of Thin Bread, also called Passover, was near. The chief priests and the teachers of the Law of Moses were looking for a way to get rid of Jesus, because they were afraid of what the people might do. Then Satan entered the heart of Judas Iscariot,* who was one of the twelve apostles.

Judas went to talk with the chief priests and the officers of the temple police about how he could help them arrest

Jesus. They were very pleased and offered to pay Judas some money. He agreed and started looking for a good chance to betray Jesus when the crowds were not around.

Jesus Washes the Feet of His Disciples

(John 13.1-20)

It was before Passover, and Jesus knew that the time had come for him to leave this world and to return to the Father. He had always loved his followers in this world, and he loved them to the very end.

Even before the evening meal started, the devil had made Judas, the son of Simon Iscariot,* decide to betray Jesus.

Jesus knew that he had come from God and would go back to God. He also knew that the Father had given him complete power. So during the meal Jesus got up, removed his outer garment, and wrapped a towel around his waist. He put some water into a large bowl. Then he began washing his disciples' feet and drying them with the towel he was wearing.

But when he came to Simon Peter, that disciple asked, "Lord, are you going to wash my feet?"

Jesus answered, "You don't really know what I am doing, but later you will understand."

"You will never wash my feet!" Peter replied.

"If I don't wash you," Jesus told him, "you don't really belong to me."

Peter said, "Lord, don't wash just my feet. Wash my hands and my head."

Jesus answered, "People who have bathed and are clean all over need to wash just their feet. And you, my disciples, are clean, except for one of you." Jesus knew who would betray him. That is why he said, "except for one of you."

After Jesus had washed his disciples' feet and had put his outer garment back on, he sat down again.* Then he said:

> Do you understand what I have done? You call me your teacher and Lord, and you should, because that is who I am. And if your Lord and teacher has washed your feet, you should do the same for each other. I have set the example, and you should do for each other exactly what I have done for you. I tell

you for certain that servants are not greater than their master, and messengers are not greater than the one who sent them. You know these things, and God will bless you, if you do them.

I am not talking about all of you. I know the ones I have chosen. But what the Scriptures say must come true. And they say, "The man who ate with me has turned against me!" I am telling you this before it all happens. Then when it does happen, you will believe who I am.* I tell you for certain that anyone who welcomes my messengers also welcomes me, and anyone who welcomes me welcomes the one who sent me.

Jesus Tells What Will Happen to Him
(John 13.21-30)

After Jesus had said these things, he was deeply troubled and told his disciples, "I tell you for certain that one of you will betray me." They were confused about what he meant. And they just stared at each other.

Jesus' favorite disciple was sitting next to him at the meal, and Simon motioned for that disciple to find out which one Jesus meant. So the disciple leaned toward Jesus and asked, "Lord, which one of us are you talking about?"

Jesus answered, "I will dip this piece of bread in the sauce and give it to the one I was talking about."

Then Jesus dipped the bread and gave it to Judas, the son of Simon Iscariot.* Right then Satan took control of Judas.

Jesus said, "Judas, go quickly and do what you have to do." No one at the meal understood what Jesus meant. But because Judas was in charge of the money, some of them thought that Jesus had told him to buy something they needed for the festival. Others thought that Jesus had told him to give some money to the poor. Judas took the piece of bread and went out.

It was already night.

The Lord's Supper
(Mark 14.22-26)

During the meal Jesus took some bread in his hands. He blessed the bread and broke it. Then he gave it to his disciples and said, "Take this. It is my body."

Jesus picked up a cup of wine and gave thanks to God. He then gave it to his disciples and said, "Drink it!" So they all drank some. Then he said, "This is my blood, which is poured out for many people, and with it God makes his agreement. From now on I will not drink any wine, until I drink new wine in God's kingdom." Then they sang a hymn and went out to the Mount of Olives.

Peter's Promise
(Mark 14.27-31)

Jesus said to his disciples, "All of you will reject me, as the Scriptures say,

'I will strike down
the shepherd,
and the sheep
will be scattered.'

But after I am raised to life, I will go ahead of you to Galilee."

Peter spoke up, "Even if all the others reject you, I never will!"

Jesus replied, "This very night before a rooster crows twice, you will say three times that you don't know me."

But Peter was so sure of himself that he said, "Even if I have to die with you, I will never say that I don't know you!"

All the others said the same thing.

Jesus Is the Way to the Father
(John 14.1-7)

Jesus said to his disciples, "Don't be worried! Have faith in God and have faith in me.* There are many rooms in my Father's house. I wouldn't tell you this, unless it was true. I am going there to prepare a place for each of you. After I have done this, I will come back and take you with me. Then we will be together. You know the way to where I am going."

Thomas said, "Lord, we don't even know where you are going! How can we know the way?"

"I am the way, the truth, and the life!" Jesus answered. "Without me, no one can go to the Father. If you had known me, you would have known the Father. But from now on, you do know him, and you have seen him."

Jesus Prays
(Luke 22.39-46)

Jesus went out to the Mount of Olives, as he often did, and his disciples went with him. When they got there, he told them, "Pray that you will not be tested."

Jesus walked on a little way before he kneeled down and prayed, "Father, if you will, please don't make me suffer by having me drink from this cup.* But do what you want, and not what I want."

Then an angel from heaven came to help him. Jesus was in great pain and prayed so sincerely that his sweat fell to the ground like drops of blood.*

Jesus got up from praying and went over to his disciples. They were asleep and worn out from being so sad. He said to them, "Why are you asleep? Wake up and pray that you will not be tested."

Jesus Is Arrested

(Luke 22.47-53)

While Jesus was still speaking, a crowd came up. It was led by Judas, one of the twelve apostles. He went over to Jesus and greeted him with a kiss.*

Jesus asked Judas, "Are you betraying the Son of Man with a kiss?"

When Jesus' disciples saw what was about to happen, they asked, "Lord, should we attack them with a sword?" One of the disciples even struck at the high priest's servant with his sword and cut off the servant's right ear.

"Enough of that!" Jesus said. Then he touched the servant's ear and healed it.

Jesus spoke to the chief priests, the temple police, and the leaders who had come to arrest him. He said, "Why

do you come out with swords and clubs and treat me like a criminal? I was with you everyday in the temple, and you didn't arrest me. But this is your time, and darkness* is in control."

Jesus Is Questioned by the Jewish Council
(Matthew 26.57-68)

After Jesus had been arrested, he was led off to the house of Caiaphas the high priest. The nation's leaders and the teachers of the Law of Moses were meeting there. But Peter followed along at a distance and came to the courtyard of the high priest's palace. He went in and sat down with the guards to see what was going to happen.

The chief priests and the whole council wanted to put Jesus to death. So they tried to find some people who would tell lies about him in court.* But they could not find any, even though many did come and tell lies. At last two men came forward and said, "This man claimed that he would tear down God's temple and build it again in three days."

The high priest stood up and asked Jesus, "Why don't you say something in your own defense? Don't you hear the charges they are making against you?" But Jesus did not answer. So the high priest said, "With the living God looking on, you must tell the truth. Tell us, are you the Messiah, the Son of God?"*

"That is what you say!" Jesus answered. "But I tell all of you,

> 'Soon you will see
> the Son of Man
> sitting at the right side*
> of God All-Powerful
> and coming on the clouds
> of heaven.'"

The high priest then tore his robe and said, "This man claims to be God! We don't need any more witnesses? You have heard what he said. What do you think?"

They answered, "He is guilty and deserves to die!" Then they spit in his face and hit him with their fists. Others slapped him and said, "You think you are the Messiah! So tell us who hit you!"

Peter Says He Does Not Know Jesus

(Matthew 26.69-75)

While Peter was sitting out in the courtyard, a servant girl came up to him and said, "You were with Jesus from Galilee."

But in front of everyone Peter said, "That's not so! I don't know what you are talking about!"

When Peter had gone out to the gate, another servant girl saw him and said to some people there, "This man was with Jesus from Nazareth."

Again Peter denied it, and this time he swore, "I don't even know that man!"

A little while later some people standing there walked over to Peter and said, "We know that you are one of them. We can tell it because you talk like someone from Galilee."

Peter began to curse and swear, "I don't know that man!"

Right then a rooster crowed, and Peter remembered that Jesus had said, "Before a rooster crows, you will say three times that you don't know me." Then Peter went out and cried hard.

Pilate Questions Jesus
(Mark 15.1-5)

Early the next morning the chief priests, the nation's leaders, and the teachers of the Law of Moses met together with the whole Jewish council. They tied up Jesus and led him off to Pilate.

He asked Jesus, "Are you the king of the Jews?"

"Those are your words," Jesus answered.

The chief priests brought many charges against Jesus. Then Pilate questioned him again, "Don't you have anything to say? Don't you hear what crimes they say you have done?" But Jesus did not answer, and Pilate was amazed.

The Death Sentence

(Mark 15.6-15)

During Passover, Pilate always freed one prisoner chosen by the people. And at that time there was a prisoner named Barabbas. He and some others had been arrested for murder during a riot. The Jewish people now came and asked Pilate to set a prisoner free, just as he usually did.

Pilate asked them, "Do you want me to free the king of the Jews?" Pilate knew that the chief priests had brought Jesus to him because they were jealous.

But the chief priests told the crowd to ask Pilate to free Barabbas. Then Pilate asked the crowd, "What do you want me to do with this man you say is* the king of the Jews?"

They yelled, "Nail him to a cross!"

Pilate asked, "But what crime has he done?"

"Nail him to a cross!" they yelled even louder.

Pilate wanted to please the crowd. So he set Barabbas free. Then he ordered his soldiers to beat Jesus with a whip and nail him to a cross.

Soldiers Make Fun of Jesus
(Mark 15.16-19)

The soldiers led Jesus inside the courtyard of the fortress* and called together the rest of the troops. They put a purple robe* on him, and on his head they placed a crown that they had made out of thorn branches. They made fun of Jesus and shouted, "Hey, you king of the Jews!" Then they beat him on the head with a stick. They spit on him and kneeled down and pretended to worship him.

Jesus Is Nailed to a Cross
(John 19.16b-27)

Jesus was taken away, and he carried his cross to a place known as "The Skull."* In Aramaic this place is called "Golgotha." There Jesus was nailed to the cross, and on each side of him a man was also nailed to a cross.

Pilate ordered the charge against Jesus to be written on a board and put above the cross. It read, "Jesus of Nazareth, King of the Jews." The words were written in Hebrew, Latin, and Greek.

The place where Jesus was taken was not far from the city, and many of the Jewish people read the charge against him. So the chief priests went to Pilate and said, "Why did you write that he is King of the Jews? You should have written, 'He claimed to be King of the Jews.'"

But Pilate told them, "What is written will not be changed!"

After the soldiers had nailed Jesus to the cross, they divided up his clothes into four parts, one for each of them. But his outer garment was made from a single piece of cloth, and it did not have any seams. The soldiers said to each other, "Let's not rip it apart. We'll gamble to see who gets it." This happened so that the Scriptures would come true, which say,

"They divided up my clothes
and gambled
for my garments."
The soldiers then did what they had decided.

Jesus' mother stood beside his cross with her sister and Mary the wife of Clopas. Mary Magdalene was standing there too.* When Jesus saw his mother and his favorite disciple with her, he said to his mother, "This man is now your son." Then he said to the disciple, "She is now your mother." From then on, that disciple took her into his own home.

The Death of Jesus
(Matthew 27.45-56)

At noon the sky turned dark and stayed that way until three o'clock. Then about that time Jesus shouted, "Eli, Eli, lema sabachthani?"* which means, "My God, my God, why have you deserted me?"

Some of the people standing there heard Jesus and said, "He's calling for Elijah."* One of them at once ran and grabbed a sponge. He soaked it in wine, then put it on a stick and held it up to Jesus.

Others said, "Wait! Let's see if Elijah will come* and save him." Once again Jesus shouted, and then he died.

At once the curtain in the temple* was torn in two from top to bottom. The earth shook, and rocks split apart. Graves opened, and many of God's people were raised to life. Then after Jesus had risen to life, they came out of their graves and went into the holy city, where many people saw them.

The officer and the soldiers guarding Jesus felt the earthquake and saw everything else that happened. They were frightened and said, "This man really was God's Son!"

Many women were looking on from a distance. They had come with Jesus from Galilee to be of help to him. Mary Magdalene, Mary the mother of James and Joseph, and the mother of James and John* were some of these women.

Jesus Is Buried
(Matthew 27.57-66)

That evening a rich disciple named Joseph from the town of Arimathea went and asked for Jesus' body. Pilate gave orders for it to be given to Joseph, who took the body and wrapped it in a clean linen cloth. Then Joseph put the body in his own tomb that had been cut into solid rock* and had never been used. He rolled a big stone against the entrance to the tomb and went away.

All this time Mary Magdalene and the other Mary were sitting across from the tomb.

On the next day, which was a Sabbath, the chief priests and the Pharisees went together to Pilate. They said, "Sir, we remember what that liar said while he was still alive. He claimed that in three days he would come back from death. So please order the tomb to be carefully guarded for three days. If you don't, his disciples may come and steal his body. They will tell the people that he has been raised to life, and this last lie will be worse than the first one."*

Pilate said to them, "All right, take some of your soldiers and guard the tomb as well as you know how." So they sealed it tight and placed soldiers there to guard it.

Jesus Is Alive

(John 20.1-10)

On Sunday morning while it was still dark, Mary Magdalene went to the tomb and saw that the stone had been rolled away from the entrance. She ran to Simon Peter and to Jesus' favorite disciple and said, "They have taken the Lord from the tomb! We don't know where they have put him."

Peter and the other disciple started for the tomb. They ran side by side, until the other disciple ran faster than Peter and got there first. He bent over and saw the strips of linen cloth lying inside the tomb, but he did not go in.

When Simon Peter got there, he went into the tomb and saw the strips of cloth. He also saw the piece of cloth

that had been used to cover Jesus' face. It was rolled up and in a place by itself. The disciple who got there first then went into the tomb, and when he saw it, he believed. At that time Peter and the other disciple did not know that the Scriptures said Jesus would rise to life. So the two of them went back to the other disciples.

Jesus Appears to Mary Magdalene
(John 20.11-18)

Mary Magdalene stood crying outside the tomb. She was still weeping, when she stooped down and saw two angels inside. They were dressed in white and were sitting where Jesus' body had been. One was at the head and the other was at the foot. The angels asked Mary, "Why are you crying?"

She answered, "They have taken away my Lord's body! I don't know where they have put him."

As soon as Mary said this, she turned around and saw Jesus standing there. But she did not know who he was. Jesus asked her, "Why are you crying? Who are you looking for?"

She thought he was the gardener and said, "Sir, if you have taken his body away, please tell me, so I can go and get him."

Then Jesus said to her, "Mary!"

She turned and said to him, "Rabboni." The Aramaic word "Rabboni" means "Teacher."

Jesus told her, "Don't hold on to me! I have not yet gone to the Father. But tell my disciples that I am going to the one who is my Father and my God, as well as your Father and your God." Mary Magdalene then went and told the disciples that she had seen the Lord. She also told them what he had said to her.

Jesus Appears to Two Disciples

(Luke 24.13-35)

That same day two of Jesus' disciples were going to the village of Emmaus, which was about seven miles from Jerusalem. As they were talking and thinking about what had happened, Jesus came near and started walking along beside them. But they did not know who he was.

Jesus asked them, "What were you talking about as you walked along?"

The two of them stood there looking sad and gloomy. Then the one named Cleopas asked Jesus, "Are you the only person from Jerusalem who didn't know what was happening there these last few days?"

"What do you mean?" Jesus asked.

They answered:

Those things that happened to Jesus from Nazareth. By what he did and said he showed that he was a powerful prophet, who pleased God and all the people. Then the chief priests and our leaders had him arrested and sentenced to die on a cross. We had hoped that he would be the one to set Israel free! But it has already been three days since all this happened.

Some women in our group surprised us. They had gone to the tomb early in the morning, but did not find the body of Jesus. They came back, saying that they had seen a vision of angels who told them that he is alive. Some men from our group went to the tomb and found it just as the women had said. But they didn't see Jesus either.

Then Jesus asked the two disciples, "Why can't you understand? How can you be so slow to believe all that the prophets said? Didn't you know that the Messiah would have to suffer before he was given his glory?" Jesus then explained

everything written about himself in the Scriptures, beginning with the Law of Moses and the Books of the Prophets.*

When the two of them came near the village where they were going, Jesus seemed to be going farther. They begged him, "Stay with us! It's already late, and the sun is going down." So Jesus went into the house to stay with them.

After Jesus sat down to eat, he took some bread. He blessed it and broke it. Then he gave it to them. At once they knew who he was, but he disappeared. They said to each other, "When he talked with us along the road and explained the Scriptures to us, didn't it warm our hearts?" So they got right up and returned to Jerusalem.

The two disciples found the eleven apostles and the others gathered together. And they learned from the group that the Lord was really alive and had appeared to Peter. Then the disciples from Emmaus told what happened on the road and how they knew he was the Lord when he broke the bread.

Jesus Appears to His Disciples
(John 20.19-23)

The disciples were afraid of the Jewish leaders, and on the evening of that same Sunday they locked themselves in a room. Suddenly, Jesus appeared in the middle of the group. He greeted them and showed them his hands and his side. When the disciples saw the Lord, they became very happy.

After Jesus had greeted them again, he said, "I am sending you, just as the Father has sent me." Then he breathed on them and said, "Receive the Holy Spirit. If you forgive anyone's sins, they will be forgiven. But if you don't forgive their sins, they will not be forgiven."

Jesus and Thomas

(John 20.24-29)

Although Thomas the Twin was one of the twelve disciples, he was not with the others when Jesus appeared to them. So they told him, "We have seen the Lord!"

But Thomas said, "First, I must see the nail scars in his hands and touch them with my finger. I must put my hand where the spear went into his side. I won't believe unless I do this!"

A week later the disciples were together again. This time Thomas was with them. Jesus came in while the doors were still locked and stood in the middle of the group. He

greeted his disciples and said to Thomas, "Put your finger here and look at my hands! Put your hand into my side. Stop doubting and have faith!"

Thomas replied, "You are my Lord and my God!"

Jesus said, "Thomas, do you have faith because you have seen me? The people who have faith in me without seeing me are the ones who are really blessed!"

Jesus Appears to Seven Disciples
(John 21.1-14)

Jesus later appeared to his disciples along the shore of Lake Tiberias. Simon Peter, Thomas the Twin, Nathanael from Cana in Galilee, and the two sons of Zebedee,* were there, together with two other disciples. Simon Peter said, "I'm going fishing!"

The others said, "We'll go with you." They went out in their boat. But they didn't catch a thing that night.

Early the next morning Jesus stood on the shore, but the disciples did not realize who he was. Jesus shouted, "Friends, have you caught anything?"

"No!" they answered.

So he told them, "Let your net down on the right side of your boat, and you will catch some fish."

They did, and the net was so full of fish that they could not drag it up into the boat.

Jesus' favorite disciple told Peter, "It's the Lord!" When Simon heard that it was the Lord, he put on the clothes that he had taken off while he was working. Then he jumped into the water. The boat was only about a hundred yards from shore. So the other disciples stayed in the boat and dragged in the net full of fish.

When the disciples got out of the boat, they saw some bread and a charcoal fire with fish on it. Jesus told his disciples, "Bring some of the fish you just caught." Simon Peter got back into the boat and dragged the net to shore. In it were one hundred fifty-three large fish, but still the net did not rip.

Jesus said, "Come and eat!" But none of the disciples dared ask who he was. They knew he was the Lord. Jesus took the bread in his hands and gave some of it to his disciples. He did the same with the fish. This was the third time that Jesus appeared to his disciples after he was raised from death.

Jesus and Peter

(John 21.15-19)

When Jesus and his disciples had finished eating, he asked, "Simon son of John, do you love me more than the others do?"*

Simon Peter answered, "Yes, Lord, you know I do!"

"Then feed my lambs," Jesus said.

Jesus asked a second time, "Simon son of John, do you love me?"

Peter answered, "Yes, Lord, you know I love you!"

"Then take care of my sheep," Jesus told him.

Jesus asked a third time, "Simon son of John, do you love me?"

Peter was hurt because Jesus had asked him three times if he loved him. So he told Jesus, "Lord, you know everything. You know I love you."

Jesus replied, "Feed my sheep. I tell you for certain that when you were a young man, you dressed yourself and went wherever you wanted to go. But when you are old, you will hold out your hands. Then others will wrap your belt around you and lead you where you don't want to go."

Jesus said this to tell how Peter would die and bring honor to God. Then he said to Peter, "Follow me!"

What Jesus' Followers Must Do
(Matthew 28.16-20)

Jesus' eleven disciples went to a mountain in Galilee, where Jesus had told them to meet him. They saw him and worshiped him, but some of them doubted.

Jesus came to them and said:

I have been given all authority in heaven and on earth! Go to the people of all nations and make them my disciples. Baptize them in the name of the Father, the Son, and the Holy Spirit, and teach them to do everything I have told you. I will be with you always, even until the end of the world.

Jesus Returns to Heaven
(Luke 24.50-53)

Jesus led his disciples out to Bethany, where he raised his hands and blessed them. As he was doing this, he left and was taken up to heaven.* After his disciples had worshiped him,* they returned to Jerusalem and were very happy. They spent their time in the temple, praising God.

NOTES(*)

1   **put it out:** Or "understood it."

3   **Abijah . . . Aaron:** The Jewish priests were divided into two groups, and one of these groups was named after Abijah. Each group served in the temple once a year for two weeks at a time. Aaron, the brother of Moses, was the first priest.

3   **burn incense:** This was done twice a day, once in the morning and again in the late afternoon.

3   **Elijah:** The prophet Elijah was known for his power to work miracles.

4   **keep people from looking down on me:** When a married woman could not have children, it was thought that the Lord was punishing her.

8   **good man:** Or "kind man," or "man who always did the right thing."

8   **name him Jesus:** In Hebrew the name "Jesus" means "the Lord saves."

9   **names . . . listed in record books:** This was done so that everyone could be made to pay taxes to the Emperor.

9   **Quirinius was governor of Syria:** It is known that Quirinius made a record of the people in A.D. 6 or 7. But the exact date of the record taking that Luke mentions is not known.

9   **first-born:** The Jewish people said that the first-born son in each of their families belonged to the Lord.

9   **dressed him in baby clothes:** The Greek text has "wrapped him in wide strips of cloth," which was how young babies were dressed.

10   **what the Law of Moses commands:** This refers to circumcision. It is the cutting off of skin from the private part of Jewish boys eight days after birth to show that they belong to the Lord.

12   **after her baby is born:** After a Jewish mother gave birth to a son, she was considered "unclean" and had to stay home until he was circumcised (see the note at 1.59). Then she had to stay home for another 33 days, before offering a sacrifice to the Lord.

12   **first-born:** See the third note for page 9.

14   **And now she was eighty-four years old:** Or "And now she had been a widow for eighty-four years."

14   **without eating:** The Jewish people sometimes went without eating (also called "fasting") to show their love for God and to become better followers.

14   **wise men:** People famous for studying the stars.

14   **his star in the east:** Or "his star rise."

16   **frankincense, and myrrh:** Frankincense was a valuable powder that was burned to make a sweet smell. Myrrh was a valuable sweet-smelling powder often used in perfume.

18   **He will be called a Nazarene:** The prophet who said this is not known.

20   **in my Father's house:** Or "doing my Father's work."

20   **For fifteen years:** This was either A.D. 28 or 29, and Jesus was about thirty years old (see Luke 3.23).

20   **Herod:** Herod Antipas, the son of Herod the Great.

20   **Annas and Caiaphas . . . high priests:** Annas was high priest from A.D. 6 until 15. His son-in-law Caiaphas was high priest from A.D. 18 until 37.

21   **children for Abraham:** The Jewish people thought they were God's chosen people because of God's promises to their ancestor Abraham.

21   **tax collectors:** These were usually Jewish people who paid the Romans for the right to collect taxes. They were hated by other Jews who thought of them as traitors to their country and to their religion.

21   **untie his sandals:** This was the duty of a slave.

22   **threshing fork:** After Jewish farmers had trampled out the grain, they used a large fork to pitch the grain and the husks into the air. Wind would blow away

the light husks, and the grain would fall back to the ground, where it could be gathered up.

23   **went without eating:** The Jewish people sometimes went without eating (also called "fasting") to show their love for God and to become better followers.

24   **the Prophet:** Many of the Jewish people expected God to send them a prophet who would be like Moses, but with even greater power. See Deuteronomy 18.15,18.

25   **Bethany:** An unknown village east of the Jordan with the same name as the village near Jerusalem.

26   **Peter:** The Aramaic name "Cephas" and the Greek name "Peter" each mean "rock."

27   **Moses and the Prophets:** The Jewish Scriptures, that is, the Old Testament.

27   **Israel . . . not deceitful:** Israel (meaning "a man who wrestled with God" or "a prince of God") was the name that the Lord gave to Jacob (meaning "cheater" or "deceiver"), the famous ancestor of the Jewish people.

27   **going up and coming down on the Son of Man:** When Jacob (see the note above) was running from his brother Esau, he had a dream in which he saw angels going up and down on a ladder from earth to heaven. See Genesis 32.22-32.

27   **my time has not yet come!:** The time when the true glory of Jesus would be seen, and he would be recognized as God's Son. See John 12.23.

29   **miracle:** The Greek text has "sign." In the Gospel of John the word "sign" is used for the miracle itself and as a way of pointing to Jesus as the Son of God.

29   **miracle:** See the note above.

31   **miracles:** See the note for page 29.

31   **from above:** Or "in a new way." The same Greek word is used in John 3.7,31.

32   **just as that metal snake was lifted up by Moses in the desert:** When the Lord punished the people of Israel by sending snakes to bite them, he told Moses to hold a metal snake up on a pole. Everyone who looked at the snake was cured of the snake bites. See Numbers 21.4-9.

34   **won't have anything to do with each other:** Or "won't use the same cups." The Samaritans lived in the land between Judea and Galilee. They worshiped God differently from the Jews and did not get along with them.

35   **this mountain:** Mount Gerizim, near the city of Shechem.

38   **leprosy:** In biblical times the word "leprosy" was used for many different kinds of skin diseases.

39   **after sunset:** The Sabbath was over, and a new day began at sunset.

40   **another Jewish festival:** Either the Festival of Shelters or Passover.

40   **Bethzatha:** Some manuscripts have "Bethesda" and others have "Bethsaida."

40   **pool:** Some manuscripts add, "They were waiting for the water to be stirred, because an angel from the Lord would sometimes come down and stir it. The first person to get into the pool after that would be healed."

41   **walking through some wheat fields:** It was the custom to let hungry travelers pick grains of wheat.

42   **to be his apostles:** These words are not in some manuscripts.

42   **known as the Eager One:** The Greek text has "Cananaean," which probably comes from a Hebrew word meaning "zealous" (see Luke 6.15). "Zealot" was the name later given to the members of a Jewish group which resisted and fought against the Romans.

42   **Iscariot:** This may mean "a man from Kerioth" (a place in Judea). But more probably it means "a man who was a liar" or "a man who was a betrayer."

42   **sat down:** Teachers in the ancient world, including Jewish teachers, usually sat down when they taught.

43   **They belong to the kingdom of heaven:** Or "The kingdom of heaven belongs to them."

43   **who want to obey him:** Or "who want to do right" or "who want everyone to be treated right."

43   **They belong to the kingdom of heaven:** See the first note for page 43.

44	**the Law and the Prophets:** The Jewish Scriptures, that is, the Old Testament.
45	**someone:** The Greek text has "brother," which may refer to people in general or to other followers.
46	**write out divorce papers for her:** Jewish men could divorce their wives, but the women could not divorce their husbands. The purpose of writing these papers was to make it harder for a man to divorce his wife. Before this law was made, all a man had to do was to send his wife away and say that she was no longer his wife.
46	**some terrible sexual sin:** This probably refers to the laws about the wrong kinds of marriages that are forbidden in Leviticus or to some serious sexual sin.
47	**right cheek:** A slap on the right cheek was a bad insult.
47	**two miles:** A Roman soldier had the right to force a person to carry his pack as far as one mile.
47	**tax collectors:** These were usually Jewish people who paid the Romans for the right to collect taxes. They were hated by other Jews who thought of them as traitors to their country and to their religion.
48	**don't let anyone know about it:** The Greek text has, "Don't let your left hand know what your right hand is doing."
49	**our food for today:** Or "the food that we need" or "our food for the coming day."
49	**sins . . . others:** Or "what we owe . . . what others owe."
49	**evil:** Or "the evil one," that is, the devil. Some manuscripts add, "The kingdom, the power, and the glory are yours forever. Amen."
49	**without eating:** See the note for page 23.
50	**live longer:** Or "grow taller."
50	**Solomon with all his wealth:** The Jewish people thought that Solomon was the richest person who had ever lived.
52	**the Law and the Prophets:** See the note for page 44.
56	**got ready to eat:** On special occasions the Jewish people often followed the Greek and Roman custom of lying down on their left side and leaning on their left elbow, while eating with their right hand. This is how the woman could come up behind Jesus and wash his feet (see Luke 7.38).
57	**washed my feet . . . greet me with a kiss . . . pour olive oil on my head:** Guests in a home were usually offered water so they could wash their feet, because most people either went barefoot or wore sandals and would come in the house with very dusty feet. Guests were also greeted with a kiss on the cheek, and special ones often had sweet-smelling olive oil poured on their head.
57	**saved:** Or "healed." The Greek word may have either meaning.
58	**and sisters:** These words are not in some manuscripts.
58	**sat down to teach:** Teachers in the ancient world, including Jewish teachers, usually sat down when they taught.
61	**went inside:** Or "went home."
61	**Gerasa:** Some manuscripts have "Gadara," and others have "Gergesa."
61	**graveyard:** It was thought that demons and evil spirits lived in graveyards.
63	**the ten cities known as Decapolis:** A group of ten cities east of Samaria and Galilee, where the people followed the Greek way of life.
63	**crossed Lake Galilee:** To the west side.
65	**heard:** Or "ignored."
65	**crying and making a lot of noise:** The Jewish people often hired mourners for funerals.
65	**Talitha, koum:** These words are in Aramaic, a language spoken in Palestine during the time of Jesus.
66	**shake the dust from your feet:** This was a way of showing rejection.
66	**Herod the ruler:** Herod Antipas, the son of Herod the Great (Matthew 2.1).
67	**the apostles returned to Jesus:** From the mission on which he had sent them (see 6.7,12,13).

67	**a place:** This was probably northeast of Lake Galilee (see Mark 6.45).
69	**almost a year's wages:** The Greek text has "two hundred silver coins." Each coin was the average day's wage for a worker.
69	**small loaves of bread:** These would have been flat and round or in the shape of a bun.
69	**back across the lake:** To the west side.
72	**miracles:** The Greek text has "signs" here and "sign" in verse 30. See the note for page 29.
72	**manna:** When the people of Israel were wandering through the desert, the Lord gave them a special kind of food to eat. It tasted like a wafer and was called "manna," which in Hebrew means, "What is this?"
73	**the last day:** When God will judge all people.
73	**manna:** See the second note for page 72.
74	**Canaanite woman:** This woman was not Jewish.
74	**Son of David:** The Jewish people expected the Messiah to be from the family of King David, and for this reason the Messiah was often called the "Son of David."
75	**feed it to dogs:** The Jewish people sometimes referred to Gentiles as dogs.
75	**Elijah:** Many of the Jewish people expected the prophet Elijah to come and prepare the way for the Messiah.
79	**My time hasn't yet come:** See the fourth note for page 27.
80	**one miracle:** The healing of the lame man (5.1-18). See the note for page 29.
81	**his time had not yet come:** See the fourth note for page 27.
81	**miracles:** See the note for page 29.
81	**had not yet been given his full glory:** In the Gospel of John, Jesus is given his full glory both when he is nailed to the cross and when he is raised from death to sit beside his Father in heaven.
82	**sat down:** See the fourth note for page 42.
82	**don't sin anymore:** Verses 1-11 are not in some manuscripts. In other manuscripts these verses are placed after John 7.36 or after John 21.25 or after Luke 21.38, with some differences in the text.
84	**miracle:** See the note for page 29.
90	**temple helper:** A man from the tribe of Levi, whose job it was to work around the temple.
90	**olive oil and wine:** In New Testament times these were used as medicine. Sometimes olive oil is a symbol for healing by means of a miracle (James 5.14).
96	**Tax collectors:** See the second note for page 21.
97	**pigs:** The Jewish religion taught that pigs were not fit to eat or even to touch. A Jewish man would have felt terribly insulted if he had to feed pigs, much less eat with them.
97	**what the pigs were eating:** The Greek text has "(bean) pods," which came from a tree in Palestine. These were used to feed animals. Poor people sometimes ate them too.
98	**ring . . . sandals:** These show that the young man's father fully accepted him as his son. A ring was a sign of high position in the family. Sandals showed that he was a son instead of a slave, since slaves did not usually wear sandals.
99	**the place of honor next to Abraham:** The Jewish people thought that heaven would be a banquet that God would give for them. Abraham would be the most important person there, and the guest of honor would sit next to him.
99	**hell:** The Greek text has "hades," which the Jewish people often thought of as the place where the dead wait for the final judgment.
100	**Moses and the prophets:** The Jewish Scriptures, that is, the Old Testament.
102	**the last day:** When God will judge all people.
105	**leprosy:** See the note for page 38.

105	**show yourselves to the priests:** People with leprosy had to be examined by a priest and told that they were well (that is "clean") before they could once again live a normal life in the Jewish community.
107	**into the temple to pray:** Jewish people usually prayed there early in the morning and late in the afternoon.
107	**tax collector:** See the second note for page 21.
107	**stood over by himself and prayed:** Some manuscripts have "stood up and prayed to himself."
107	**without eating:** See the note for page 23.
107	**People who are like these little children belong to the kingdom of God:** Or "The kingdom of God belongs to people who are like these little children."
110	**mother of James and John:** The Greek text has "mother of the sons of Zebedee." See Matthew 26.37.
110	**right side . . . left:** The most powerful people in a kingdom sat at the right and left side of the king.
110	**drink from the cup:** In the Scriptures a cup is sometimes used as a symbol of suffering. To "drink from the cup" is to suffer.
110	**rescue:** The Greek word often, though not always, means the payment of a price to free a slave or a prisoner.
111	**in charge of collecting taxes:** See the second note for page 21.
112	**pay back four times as much:** Both Jewish and Roman law said that a person must pay back four times the amount that was taken.
112	**saved:** Zacchaeus was Jewish, but it is only now that he is rescued from sin and placed under God's care.
112	**son of Abraham:** As used in this verse, the words mean that Zacchaeus is truly one of God's special people.
113	**The Lord:** Or "the master of the donkeys."
114	**spread clothes . . . put down branches:** This was one way that the Jewish people welcomed a famous person.
115	**Hooray:** This translates a word that can mean "please save us." But it is most often used as a shout of praise to God.
115	**Son of David:** See the second note for page 74.
117	**to meet the groom:** Some manuscripts add "and the bride." It was the custom for the groom to go to the home of the bride's parents to get his bride. Young girls and other guests would then go with them to the home of the groom's parents, where the wedding feast would take place.
118	**Iscariot:** See the third note for page 42.
120	**Iscariot:** See the third note for page 42.
120	**sat down again:** On special occasions the Jewish people followed the Greek and Roman custom of lying down on their left side and leaning on their left elbow, while eating with their right hand.
121	**I am:** For the Jewish people the most holy name of God is "Yahweh," which may be translated "I am." In the Gospel of John "I am" is sometimes used by Jesus to show that he is that one.
121	**Iscariot:** See the third note for page 42.
124	**Have faith in God and have faith in me:** Or "You have faith in God, so have faith in me."
124	**having me drink from this cup:** In the Scriptures "to drink from a cup" sometimes means to suffer.
124	**Then an angel . . . like drops of blood:** Verses 43,44 are not in some manuscripts.
125	**greeted him with a kiss:** It was the custom for people to greet each other with a kiss on the cheek.
127	**darkness:** Darkness stands for the power of the devil.
127	**some people who would tell lies about him in court:** The Law of Moses taught that two witnesses were necessary before a person could be put to death. See verse 60.

127	**Son of God:** One of the titles used for the kings of Israel.
127	**right side:** The place of power and honor.
131	**this man you say is:** These words are not in some manuscripts.
132	**fortress:** The place where the Roman governor stayed. It was probably at Herod's palace west of Jerusalem, though it may have been Fortress Antonio, north of the temple, where the Roman troops were stationed.
132	**purple robe:** This was probably a Roman soldier's robe.
132	**"The Skull":** The place was probably given this name because it was near a large rock in the shape of a human skull.
134	**Jesus' mother stood beside his cross with her sister and Mary the wife of Clopas. Mary Magdalene was standing there too:** The Greek text may also be understood to include only three women ("Jesus' mother stood beside the cross with her sister, Mary the mother of Clopas. Mary Magdalene was standing there too.") or merely two women ("Jesus' mother was standing there with her sister Mary of Clopas, that is Mary Magdalene."). "Of Clopas" may mean "daughter of" or "mother of."
134	**Eli . . . sabachthani:** These words are in Aramaic, a language spoken in Palestine during the time of Jesus.
134	**Elijah:** In Aramaic the name "Elijah" sounds like "Eli," which means "my God."
134	**Elijah will come:** Many of the Jewish people expected the prophet Elijah to come and prepare the way for the Messiah.
134	**curtain in the temple:** There were two curtains in the temple. One was at the entrance, and the other separated the holy place from the most holy place that the Jewish people thought of as God's home on earth. The second curtain is probably the one that is meant.
135	**of James and John:** The Greek text has "of Zebedee's sons." See Matthew 26.37.
135	**tomb . . . solid rock:** Some of the Jewish people buried their dead in rooms carved into solid rock. A heavy stone was rolled against the entrance.
135	**the first one:** Probably the belief that Jesus is the Messiah.
140	**the Law of Moses and the Books of the Prophets:** The Jewish Scriptures, that is, the Old Testament.
142	**the two sons of Zebedee:** James and John.
143	**more than the others do?:** Or "more than you love these things?"
145	**and was taken up to heaven:** These words are not in some manuscripts.
145	**After his disciples had worshiped him:** These words are not in some manuscripts.